CORNERSTONE to Cupola

CORNERSTONE to Cupola

The Ohio Statehouse

Chris Matheney

Orange frazer Press
Wilmington, Ohio

ISBN 978-1939710-666

Copyright©2017 Capitol Square Review and Advisory Board

No part of this publication may be reproduced in any material form (including photocopying or storing in any medium by electronic means and whether or not transiently or incidentally to some other use of this publication) without the written permission of the copyright holder except in accordance with the provisions of the Copyright, Designs and Patents Act 1988.

Published for Capitol Square Review and Advisory Board by:
Orange Frazer Press
P.O. Box 214
Wilmington, OH 45177
Telephone: 937.382.3196 for price and shipping information.
Website: www.orangefrazer.com

Book and cover design: Alyson Rua and Orange Frazer Press

Cover photograph by Richard W. Burry

Library of Congress Control Number: 2017943499

First Printing

Limited Edition

Printed in the United States

Sources:

Cummings, A. L. (1948), *Ohio's Capitols At Columbus*. Unpublished manuscript.

Martin, William T. *History of Franklin County.* Columbus: Follet, Foster & Company, 1858. Print.

Schooley Caldwell Associates. *The Ohio Statehouse Master Plan*. Columbus: Schooley Caldwell Associates, 1989.

Taylor, W. A. *Ohio Statesmen And Hundred Year Book.* Columbus: Westbote Company, 1892. Print.

Acknowledgments

Capitol Square Review and Advisory Board
Representative Clifford A. Rosenberger, Speaker of
 the Ohio House of Representatives
Senator Bob Peterson, Senate President Pro Tempore
Laura Battocletti, Executive Director
Dayna Jalkanen, Deputy Director of Museum and Education
Katie Montgomery, Educational Services &
 Museum Collections Manager
Erin Haar, Museum and Programs Coordinator
Christopher Landers, Museum Assistant
Michael Rupert, Communications Specialist

New York State Library
Victor DesRosiers, Manuscripts and Special Collections

Ohio Government Telecommunications
Dan Shellenbarger, Executive Director

Ohio History Connection
Lily Birkhimer, Digital Projects Coordinator
Cheryl J. Straker, Project Coordinator
Lisa Wood, Curator for Visual Resources &
 History Services Unit Manager

Ohio House of Representatives
Mike Dittoe, Chief of Staff
Mike Elicson, Digital Media Manager

Ohio Senate
Rob Abel, Director of Digital Media

Schooley Caldwell Associates—Architect of the Capitol
Robert D. Loversidge, Jr., FAIA, President/CEO

State Library of Ohio
Cindy McLaughlin, former Deputy State Librarian
 for Library Services
Marsha McDevitt-Stredney, Ph.D., Director,
 Marketing & Communications

Toledo Museum of Art
Julia Hayes, Systems Analyst/Imaging Specialist

Richard W. Burry

John and Janet Waldsmith

Finally, I wish to express with deep gratitude, my thanks to Abbott Lowell Cummings of South Deerfield, Massachusetts, for his early research on the Ohio Statehouse. Working under a special grant from the Ohio Legislature from 1946–1948, Cummings completed a very thorough study of the construction of the Ohio Statehouse which laid the groundwork for future research on the subject. In the preface to his unpublished study entitled: *Ohio's Capitols At Columbus*, Mr. Cummings lamented that few of the early reports of the different builders had been preserved, and that the plans that are available date to later phases of the work. Unstinted, he combed through the various architect's and commissioners' reports to the legislature, as well as other pertinent reports in the legislative journals. Yet he found an *unfailing mine of information* in the early Columbus newspapers, which gave him clues and insight into the process and politics of designing and constructing Ohio's capitol buildings at Columbus. Taking that tip to heart, I have made use of many early newspaper stories to help illustrate the history of the Ohio Statehouse and Capitol Square.

—*Chris Matheney*, March 2017

This photograph shows two boys selling newspapers on the northwest corner of the Ohio Statehouse, ca. 1895–1910. The boy on the left is selling the *Citizen*; the boy on the right is selling the *Dispatch*. Newspapers from the past provide excellent insight into the history of the Ohio Statehouse and Capitol Square. *Courtesy of the Ohio History Connection.*

Photo by Mike Elicson.

Contents

ix   Foreword

3   The First Capitols

9   The Ohio Statehouse

85   The Senate Building

101   Grounds & Monuments

121   Index

125   About the Author

Photo by Mike Elicson.

Foreword

"We are not enemies, but friends. We must not be enemies. Though passion may have strained it must not break our bonds of affection. The mystic chords of memory, stretching from every battlefield and patriot grave to every living heart and hearthstone all over this broad land, will yet swell the chorus of the Union, when again touched, as surely they will be, by the better angels of our nature."

—President Abraham Lincoln

<small>From his first Inaugural Address, a passage featured prominently in the "Heart of Democracy" Exhibit at the Ohio Statehouse.</small>

IT IS HARD TO IMAGINE that shortly before construction of the Ohio Statehouse was complete, one of our nation's most storied presidents was delivering his first inaugural address and our country was on the brink of Civil War. The debate over war was waging in this extraordinary building and across our then-33 other states as to whether the United States should continue to be what our Constitution calls "a more perfect Union." As one of the oldest capitols still in use today with its unique cupola and rotunda and original artwork and furniture, the Statehouse has stood the test of time for over 150 years and has remained a treasure for generations of Ohioans.

One cannot walk through the halls of the Statehouse without seeing and feeling the presence of the countless people and events who have shaped this great state. Prior to being elected to the highest office in the land, two U.S. presidents first worked in the Statehouse as governors. And in 1920, Ohio became one of the first states to guarantee women the right to vote.

The Statehouse reminds us that around every corner we have forged a brighter future with the courage and fortitude of those who came before us. From the laying of the cornerstone of the Statehouse to today, this building has witnessed some of our country's greatest debates, from the Civil War to Civil Rights. Housed within this great structure are rooms like the Ladies Gallery, which celebrates the women who paved Ohio's beginnings and who relentlessly fought for equal rights, to the George Washington Williams Room that pays tribute to the first African-American ever elected to the Ohio state legislature.

Since its opening in 1861, the Ohio Statehouse has served as the backdrop of some of our nation's most notable events. It was in these halls that Abraham Lincoln learned he had secured enough votes in the electoral college to win the Presidency as well as addressed the legislature in the House Chamber. Sadly, the Statehouse Rotunda is also where the public had the opportunity to pay their final respects to President Lincoln and other heroes like John Glenn, the first American to orbit the earth.

Today, the Ohio Statehouse, affectionately known as "The People's House," has been restored to its original splendor, thanks to years of historic renovations. As you visit this beautiful landmark located in the heart of our capital city, I hope you, too, will develop an appreciation for the Statehouse—a building that encapsulates so much of Ohio's rich history and embodies the spirit that lies within the heart of every Ohioan.

Clifford A. Rosenberger

Speaker, Ohio House of Representatives

CORNERSTONE to *Cupola*

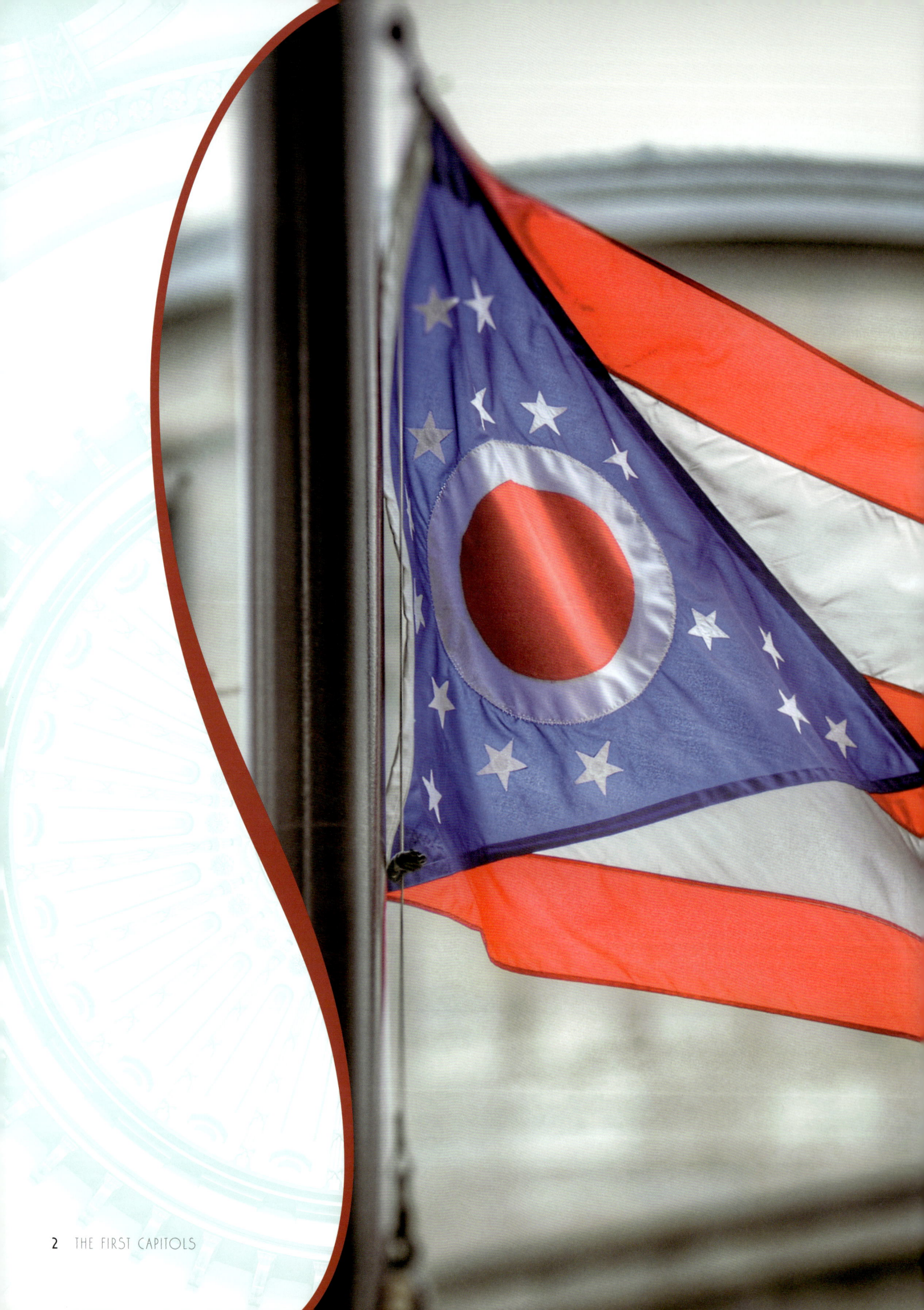

THE FIRST Capitols

Photo by Mike Elicson.

AS MUCH AS GEOGRAPHY *was the final determining factor for the location of Ohio's capitol, other factors such as political rivalries, territorial jealousy, and public controversy all played their part. The capitol of Ohio would change three times before finding its permanent home in Columbus. From 1803 to 1816 the capitol shifted from one location to the next as Ohio officially transitioned from roughhewn territory to full-fledged statehood.*

Prior to statehood, Chillicothe had served as the capitol of the eastern half of the Northwest Territory since 1800. At first, the territorial government met in a two-story log cabin built by Bazil Abrams in 1798. Known as the Abrams House, it was occupied in an official capacity by territorial judges and legislators, yet it also served the local community for religious services as well as a gambling location. Cramped conditions led to the construction of a more formal capitol for the territorial government. A stone structure designed by William Rutledge and William Guthrie and built in the federal style (which was the preferred style of state capitols at the time) was completed in 1801. This was a two-story, square building with a hipped roof and cupola. The cupola was surmounted by a sheet brass weathervane in the shape of a federal eagle, known locally as the Ohio Eagle. Although it was a vast improvement over the Abrams House, a former Chillicothe resident described it as uncomfortable, poorly lit, cold, roughly finished within, and altogether unsuited to the purposes for which it was built. Despite this description, the Chillicothe courthouse became the first Ohio Statehouse on

CORNERSTONE TO CUPOLA 3

Left: Ohio's first Statehouse in Chillicothe, Ohio, 1801, came complete with an Ohio Eagle weather vane. The two story log cabin Abrams House can be seen in the right side background of this image. *Courtesy of the Ohio History Connection.* **Right:** The Zanesville state capitol building was built in the federal style of architecture. It was torn down in the 1870s to make space for a new county courthouse. *Courtesy of the Ohio History Connection.*

March 1, 1803, when the state of Ohio officially entered the union.

Chillicothe would not hold that honor for long. The advantages of being the political center as well as the social and cultural focus of the state were attractive to other cities. The 1802 Ohio Constitution had placed the capitol at Chillicothe only until 1808; and that the legislature could not raise money for new state office buildings until 1809. This set off a competition among existing Ohio towns to host a potentially new state capitol. Towns like Worthington and Franklinton in central Ohio began to set aside portions of their land. Yet the residents of Zanesville in a show of civic pride made perhaps the shrewdest political gamble by contracting with architect James Hampson to construct a new public building in their town. Like the Chillicothe capitol building, it was constructed in the federal style, its main difference being that it was made of brick rather than stone. The gamble paid off as Zanesville became the official state capitol in December, 1809, when the legislature held its first session there. The victory was short-lived however; not long after the move to Zanesville, the representatives resolved to find a more permanent seat of government.

On February 20, 1810, state lawmakers enacted legislation that provided for a selection of a permanent site for a capitol not more than forty miles from what may be deemed the common center of the state; meaning of course, that both Chillicothe and Zanesville were completely out of the running. A five-man commission was selected to receive proposals of donations to the state toward creating public buildings and to report back on these findings. Several proposals were made from well-established towns like Lancaster (1799), Newark (1802), Delaware (1808), and Franklinton (1797). Land, buildings, and money were what these towns offered if the General Assembly would agree to make their site the new state capitol. The commission dismissed Franklinton as a possible site due to the fact that the Scioto River had flooded this low, west bank location in 1798, causing some of the residents to relocate just to survive. Lynn Starling, James Johnston, John Kerr, and Alexander McLaughlin, all prominent land owners from Franklinton made another offer to the General Assembly. They would lay out a town on the high banks of the Scioto

THE FIRST CAPITOLS

GREAT SEAL OF OHIO

In March of 1803, the first legislature in session at Chillicothe adopted a law which created the design of the Great Seal of Ohio: "On the right side, near the bottom, a sheaf of wheat and on the left a bundle of seventeen arrows, both standing erect; in the background, and rising above the sheaf and bundle of arrows a mountain, over which shall appear a rising sun, the state seal to be surrounded by these words, "The Great Seal of the State of Ohio."

A tradition that persists to this day is that the design was inspired by the view of Mt. Logan from Thomas Worthington's home Adena, in Chillicothe. The story relates that Thomas Worthington, former U.S. Senator and sixth governor of Ohio, Edward Tiffin, first governor of Ohio, and William Creighton, first secretary of state, after spending the night at Worthington's home arose the next morning to the spectacular view of the sun rising above Mt. Logan, which provided the inspiration for Ohio's Great Seal.

Inset: This stained glass Great Seal of Ohio originally hung in the Rotunda dome from the 1920s to 1965. During the renovation of Capitol Square, it was discovered stored away in the Senate Building. It now resides in the Ohio Statehouse Museum. *Photo by Mike Elicson.*
Above: The view of Mount Logan from the Great Seal Overlook at Thomas Worthington's home Adena, in Chillicothe, Ohio. *Courtesy of Adena Mansion and Gardens Society.*

CORNERSTONE TO CUPOLA   5

east of Franklinton in an area known as Wolf Ridge. The same group offered the state two ten-acre plots: one for the state capitol and one for a penitentiary. They would construct the Statehouse, additional public offices, penitentiary, and any other buildings deemed necessary by the legislature, and that these same structures would be worth $50,000 when they were completed. Finally, they offered to have everything completed by December of 1817. Working in concert with these landowners was a tavern owner and Senator from Franklinton named Joseph Foos. Senator Foos also operated a ferry on the west bank of the Scioto across from Wolf Ridge (the proposed site for the capitol) and recognized the economic opportunity of developing the area. In session in Zanesville during the early winter of 1812, Foos showed his political skills and secured the needed votes for the Wolf Ridge location. He was able to accomplish this by adding the proviso that Chillicothe would be the temporary capitol again during the construction of the new state capitol, thereby gaining the Chillicothe representatives' votes. Further, an amendment was added that the new permanent seat of government was only permanent until 1840, when the legislature could again look at the issue of moving the capitol. This was the winning formula and the legislature officially accepted the Franklinton proposal on February 14, 1812. In the final act of his legislative victory in securing the location of the capitol, evidence seems to support that Senator Foos himself suggested the name of the great explorer, Columbus, for the new seat of government. This was accepted and became law on February 21, 1812.

While the new capitol was being built under the direction of William Ludlow, state government returned to

Right: The first Columbus Statehouse followed the same school of design as the Chillicothe and Zanesville capitol buildings. The governor's office was located in the public office building along with the auditor, secretary of state, and treasurer. *Courtesy of the Ohio History Connection.* **Bottom:** William Ludlow designed the first capitol building at Columbus. He placed lintel stones above each of the entrances. This lintel stone was originally above the east entrance, and states the following: "General good, the object of Legislation, perfected by a knowledge of mans' wants, and Natures abounding means applied, by establishing principles opposed to Monopoly." —Ludlow. *Courtesy of the Ohio History Connection.*

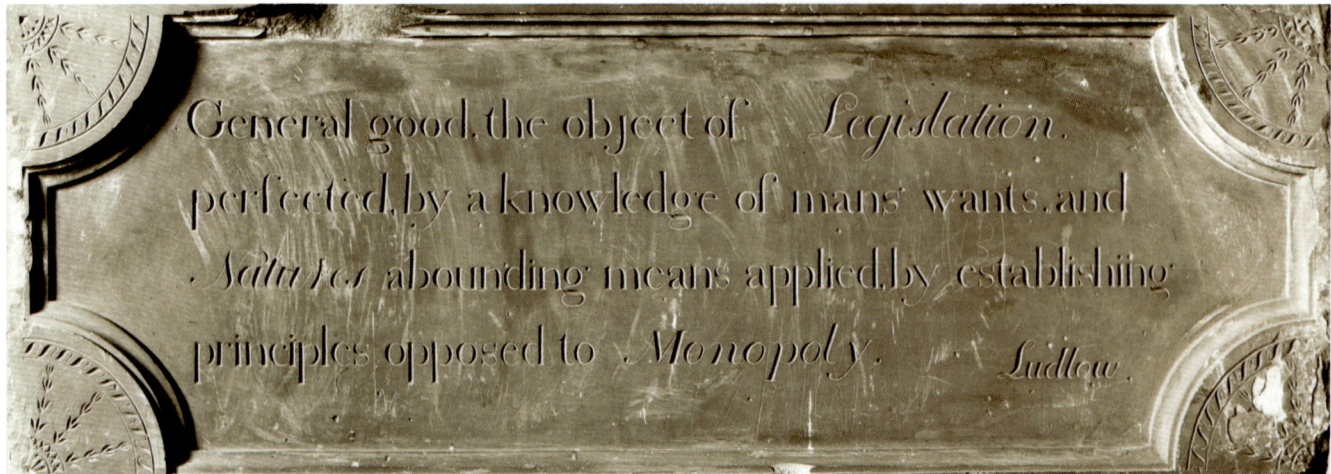

6 THE FIRST CAPITOLS

Chillicothe. The exterior of the first Statehouse in Columbus followed the same school of design as the first two capitols in Chillicothe and Zanesville. Teamsters were hired to haul the stone necessary for the foundation, door and window sills from the swampy and muddy Black Lick area, roughly fourteen miles away. The bricks used in the construction were partly made out of a beautiful mound that stood on the summit of the high ground at the intersection of High and Mound streets. William T. Martin, who had moved to Columbus in 1815, described this first Statehouse as a "common, plain brick building, seventy-five feet north and south, by fifty feet east and west on the ground, and two lofty stories high, with a square roof, that is, eaves and cornice at both sides and ends, and ascending to the balcony and steeple in the center in which was a first rate, well-toned bell. The top of the spire was one hundred and six feet from the ground. On the roof adjoining the balcony, on two sides, were neat railed walks from which a spectator might view the whole town as upon a map, and had also a fine view of the winding Scioto, and of the level country around as far as the eye could reach." (William T. Martin, *History of Franklin County* (1858) p. 334.)

This first Statehouse at Columbus was finished in the fall of 1816, and was located on the corner of State and High Streets; leaving the center of the square wide open, as if they *knew* it was only temporary. A public office building was built next door that contained the offices of the auditor and treasurer, secretary of state, governor, as well as being the location of the newly created State Library (est. 1817). The new capitol at Columbus welcomed the fifteenth General Assembly of the State of Ohio on the first Monday of December, 1816 (a full year ahead of schedule), as it began its first session. Ironically, considering all of the political maneuvering involved over the location of the state capitol, it was Chillicothe's own Thomas Worthington (6th Governor of Ohio, 1814–1818) who was the first governor of the state to take up official residence in the new Columbus Statehouse.

CLEARING THE STATEHOUSE SQUARE

"To Governor Thomas Worthington belongs the unique distinction of being the only Ohio Governor ever arrested and started to jail for debt. In 1815 or 1816, Governor Worthington contracted with Judge Jarvis Pike to grub and chop the timber off the present State House square. The Governor was a non-resident of Franklin County, residing at Chillicothe. Some misunderstanding arose as to the payment of Judge Pike for his labors, whereupon he sued out a capias from the court of 'Squire King, and had the Governor arrested and marched off to jail. He was not locked up, however, the matter having been amicably adjusted."
–Taylor, W.A., *Ohio Statesmen and Hundred Year Book*, page 529.

Portrait of Thomas Worthington as a young man, age 23, by N. Gwinn, ca. 1800. He served as one of the first United States Senators from Ohio, and as Ohio's sixth governor. Worthington is known as the Father of Ohio Statehood for his diligent work in bringing Ohio into the Union. *Courtesy of the Ohio History Connection.*

8 THE OHIO STATEHOUSE

THE OHIO Statehouse

TEMPLE OF DEMOCRACY

T*HE FACT THAT OHIO settled its matters of state so quickly is to be marveled at, especially when taking into account the War of 1812 that was demanding the attention of the country. Yet despite this seemingly benign influence on the rapid construction time of the first capitol buildings at Columbus, the war ultimately brought about an architectural shift in America's public buildings and homes.* The mid-to-late 18th century style of Federal architecture was still visible throughout the country. Roman buildings had been the original inspiration for this style, but archaeological digging in the early 19th century revealed that Greece (the birthplace of democracy) had influenced Rome with even earlier designs. Growing disaffection with England due largely to the war sparked America's interest in Grecian models

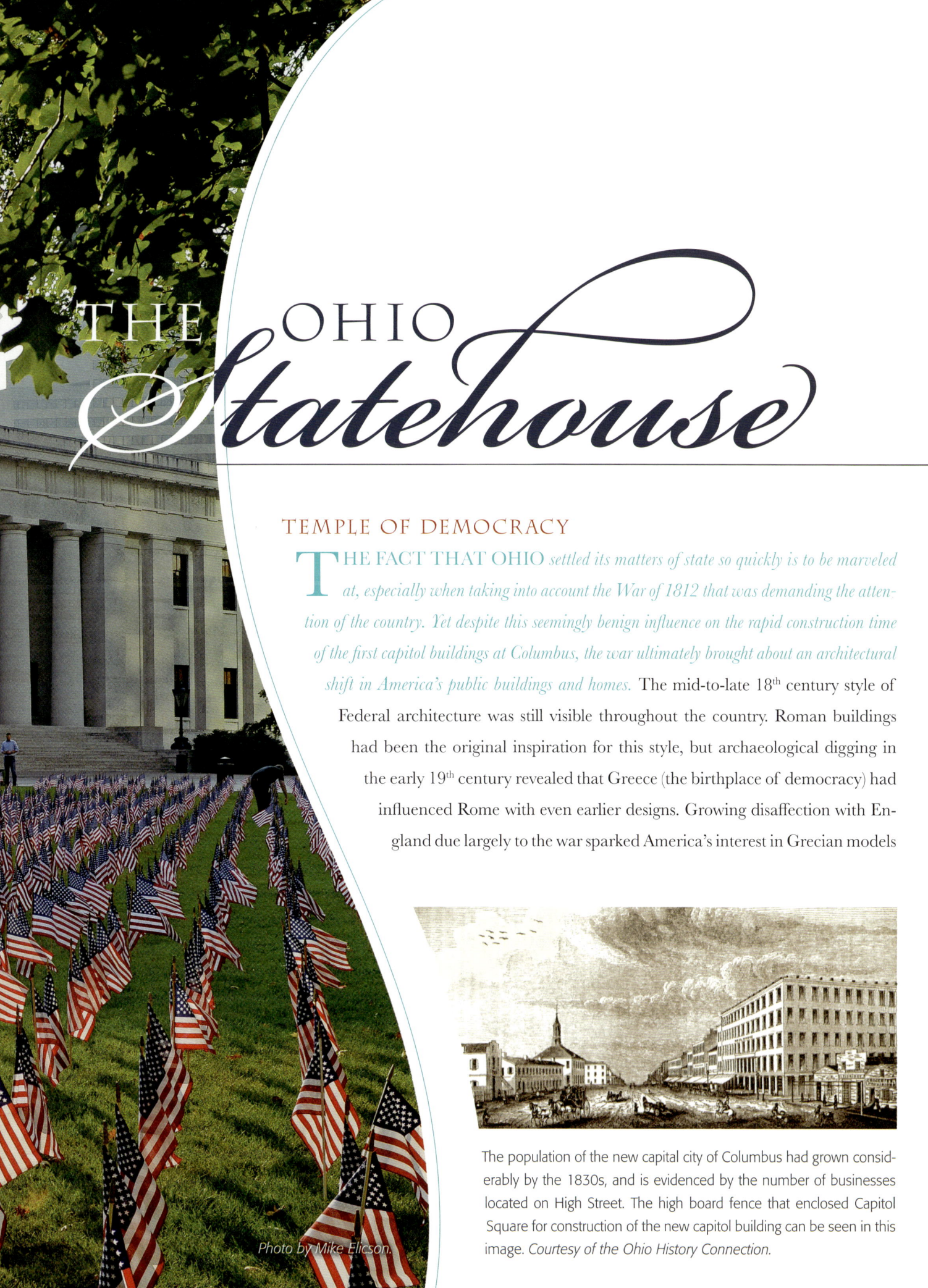

Photo by Mike Elicson.

The population of the new capital city of Columbus had grown considerably by the 1830s, and is evidenced by the number of businesses located on High Street. The high board fence that enclosed Capitol Square for construction of the new capitol building can be seen in this image. *Courtesy of the Ohio History Connection.*

CORNERSTONE TO CUPOLA   9

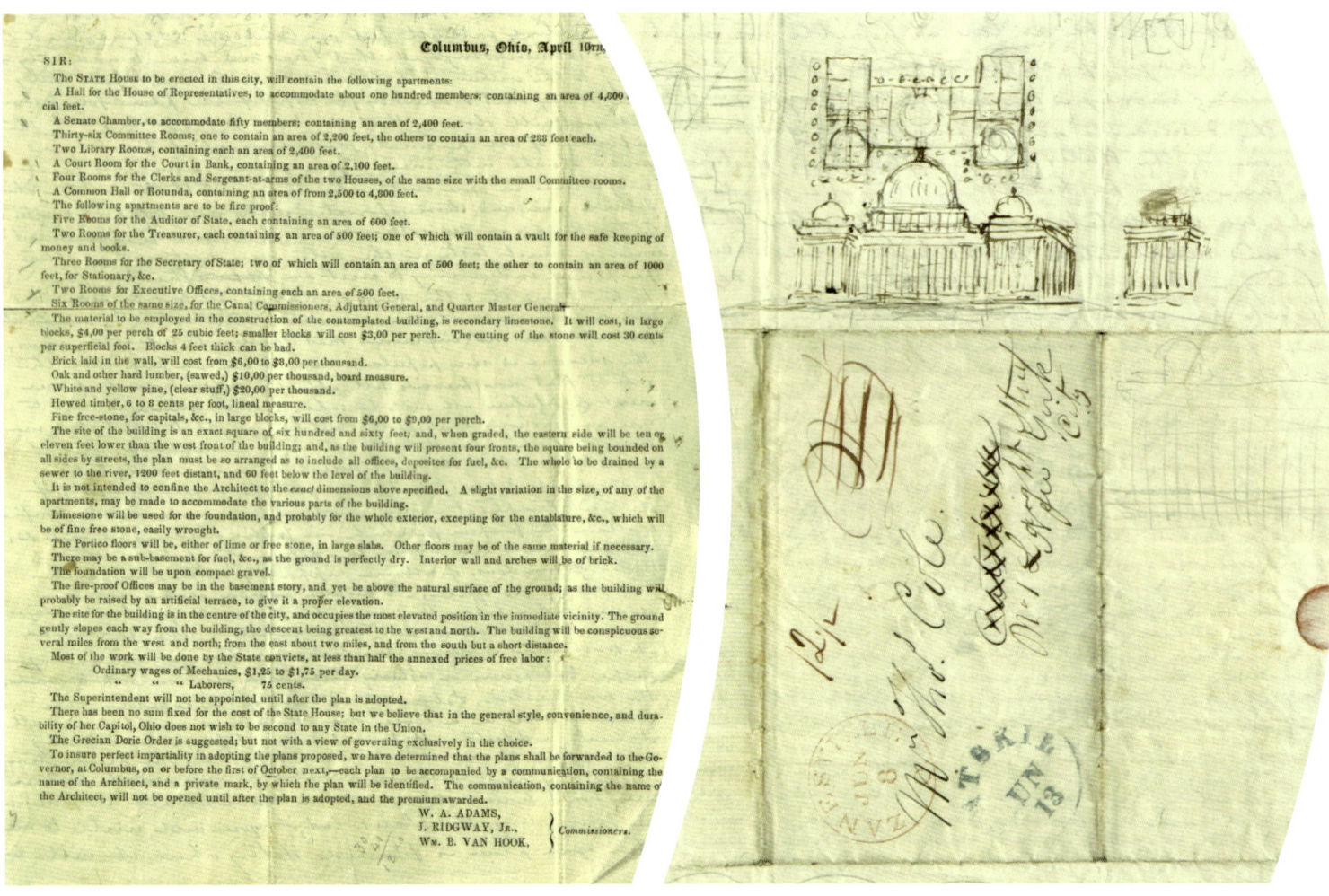

Thomas Cole's copy of the contest circular, and the initial sketch he drew of his plan for the Ohio Statehouse. Stating the rules of the contest, the circular also mentioned: "There has been no sum fixed for the cost of the State House; but we believe that in general style, convenience, and durability of her Capitol, Ohio does not wish to be second to any State in the Union." —New York State Library.

with their strong connections to classical tradition and even more important to democracy. From 1818 to 1850, Greek Revival architecture dominated the design of American public buildings and is considered the first truly national style. Nine more states had been added to the Union when Ohio decided it was time to return its capitol to the ancient and classical roots of democracy.

Hard use by an active and growing government would take its toll on the buildings of capitol square. The crowded and poorly kept condition of the buildings can be judged from the nickname they had been given by Columbus residents: *Rat Row*. A source for lively comment from the press and public, the need for larger and better buildings was being felt by government officials by the 1830s. In 1837, Governor Vance, in addressing the legislature, noted that the Ohio Penitentiary convicts had finished cutting the stone for the Central Ohio Lunatic Asylum in Columbus. Feeling that it was an excellent opportunity with so many skilled laborers he stated: "I would therefore respectfully submit whether it would be sound economy to make provision for preparing materials for a State House and public offices. Our present State Office buildings are not only inconvenient, but much exposed, and liable to destruction by fire." (Cummings. Abbot Lowell, *Ohio's Capitols at Columbus*, page 23.) This suggestion fell on receptive ears in the legislature, and a bill was passed on January 26, 1838, authorizing the construction of a new statehouse.

Three commissioners were appointed to get the project underway and they came up with a clever idea to entice some of the country's best architects to participate in the endeavor. They held a contest. The method had some precedent. The nation's capitol building in Washington D.C. began with a design competition, as had the state capitol in Harrisburg, Pennsylvania. With the approval of the legislature, the commissioners placed notices in several prominent newspapers in New York City, Philadelphia, and Cincinnati, requesting that designs for the new statehouse be submitted. Prizes in the form of cash were offered for the top three drawings. First place would receive $500, second place $300, and third place $200. For those who inquired about the contest, a circular letter was prepared that explained all of the rules of the competition. Emphasizing the Grecian Doric order as the style to be used in designing the new building, the circular also specified the material to be used: limestone for the foundation and exterior of the building. This fact suggests that the commissioners had already entered into a contract with a local landowner that allowed them to use native Ohio limestone at an attractive price. Dimensions in square footage of the various principle rooms were provided as well as a detailed description of the site. No fixed sum for the construction price had been decided on, yet the commissioners boldly noted that Ohio does not wish to be second to any state in the Union.

In all, nearly sixty designs were submitted by the October 1, 1838 deadline, including one from a New York landscape painter named Thomas Cole, who wrote to a friend when he heard about the competition: "Do you know that I'm something of an architect?" Thomas Cole would eventually place third in the competition behind Henry Walter and Martin E. Thompson who finished first and second respectively. Cole's exterior design was considered favorable, but his interior work left the commissioners feeling deflated. In a letter dated November 14, 1838, from W.A. Adams (one of the three commissioners) to Thomas Cole, Adams stated: "…we were surprised to find that you proposed to finish the interior of your plan in so cheap and unsubstantial a manner." Adams, who of course had the inside word on the top designs, ended the same letter with: "At all events you will hear from me as soon as the Legislature acts upon our report. In the meantime do not place your hopes of everlasting fame upon frail stone but look rather to imperishable paint, with this sage advice; I bid you for the present farewell." Clearly, Adams was trying to soften the blow and despite this outcome, many feel that Thomas Cole's drawing would have the most influence on the final exterior design of the new Ohio Statehouse. Upon the completion of the contest, the commissioners acknowledged they were "…governed by the views which they supposed prompted the act under which they were appointed. First, to construct an edifice which should combine in its interior arrangement perfect security to the archive of the several departments of the public service (the ever present threat of fire destroying public records being in their minds) and convenience to the several bodies and officers to be accommodated. And second, that in its exterior form and interior disposition of apartments there should unite that beauty and grandeur which the rules of art require and which comport with the dignity and wealth of state." (Remarks of the Statehouse Commissioners, 1838.) Having set out their goals, they further made it clear that "the degree of civilization and knowledge that a community possessed was most clearly to be seen in its arts, and the highest form of that expression was architecture." (Remarks of the Statehouse Commissioners, 1838.)

Clearly, the commissioners were well aware that the building they were charged with creating was more than just a roof and walls. They also stated that the building will be accomplished by the execution of any of the plans which have been awarded premiums. Faced with three designs felt equally suitable, but also possibly too expensive, the three-man committee took a step very typical of committees—to save money they decided to spend money. A prominent New York architect, Alexander Jackson Davis, was brought into the project as a consultant, and prepared drawings of each of the final entries. Davis had become a sort of specialist at state capitol consultations, having been involved in the design and construction of the capitol building in Indianapolis in 1831, and both Raleigh, North Carolina, and Springfield, Illinois, afterwards. As with his work in Columbus, none of the capitols would be the work of Davis alone, but showed his hand as a collator

The Architect's Dream by Thomas Cole, founder of the group of landscape painters known as the Hudson River School and eventual third place winner of the Ohio Statehouse design contest; was originally commissioned by architect Ithiel Town in 1839. The Toldeo Museum of Art states that the painting "portrays an ideal realm imagined by the architect, who reclines with eyes closed atop a monumental column. Arranged in historic order, the Egyptian pyramid and temple give way to Greek and Roman temples of the Doric, Ionic, and Corinthian Orders, and to the left, a Gothic cathedral." Cole fancied himself an architect in addition to being an artist, and perhaps was displaying his knowledge of classical architecture. Town eventually refused the painting, being disappointed that there wasn't enough landscape.

Thomas Cole (American, born England, 1801–1848). *The Architect's Dream*, 1840, oil on canvas, 53 x 84 1/16 in., Toledo Museum of Art (Toledo, Ohio), Purchased with funds from the Florence Scott Libbey Bequest in Memory of her Father, Maurice A. Scott, 1949.162. *Image Source, Toledo Museum of Art.*

and amender. Davis merged the concepts originated by Walter, Thompson, and Cole into a composite design that ostensibly was to blend the best features of each. In its final form, the Ohio Statehouse is a combination of the top three designs.

Upon the completion of the contest, the commissioners turned their attention to some of the more physical needs of the project. Earlier they had entered into a contract with a local quarry owner, William Sullivant, to supply all of the stone necessary for the capitol. The quarry lay about three miles west of Columbus along the Scioto River. Ohio limestone or Columbus limestone, as the state geologist refers to it, is the bedrock around central Ohio, and was used exclusively for the foundation and exterior walls of the Statehouse. "Two-thousand sixty-two perches of stone were delivered during the course of the year, part at the site of the proposed building and a part at the penitentiary where the convicts were set to work preparing it for the walls." (Cummings, ibid, page 35.) The state librarian, working in his office, saw the first stone hauled into the public square on May 16 of the same year. A workshop was established in the spring of 1839 on the square, and a high board fence was placed around the square to keep the convict labor enclosed. To admit the convicts as well as wagons carrying supplies, a gate was set up at High and Broad streets, all of this under the watchful eyes of guards who had sentry boxes placed along the perimeter of the fence. Excavations began on the square, and the placement of the massive foundation commenced under the direction of Henry Walter, architect of St. Peter's Cathedral and first place winner of the Ohio Statehouse design competition. It was at this time that delays in construction began owing to the "adjustments of the several details and modifications of the plan." (Cummings, ibid, page 36.) Adjustments and modifications would hamper the building of the new capitol throughout its twenty-two year construction span. Yet the ground was prepared, and the foundation was far enough along that all was in readiness for the placement of the cornerstone on an auspicious day— July 4, 1839.

Citizens from Columbus, as well as men, women, and children from the surrounding areas began to flood the nearby streets by eight o'clock in the morning. Jostling crowds listened to patriotic speeches, songs, and a reading of the Declaration of Independence. Veterans of the American Revolution and the War of 1812 turned out in old uniforms alongside current militia companies like the Lancaster Guards and the Black Hawk Braves. The mayor and city council were in attendance as well as state officials, who were there to oversee the celebration. Added to the festive atmosphere was the constant braying of countless horses, mules, and oxen that had drawn a number of the participants to the capitol. Roughly five thousand individuals were said to have taken part in the day's festivities, and the whole formed a procession and marched to the center of the public square. Shortly before entering the recently erected gate, a large group of Columbus mechanics that were angry with the state's decision to use convict labor to build the new statehouse, left the procession and held their own demonstrations just a short distance away.

"Let the foundations be deep and strong; let the materials be of nature's most lasting gifts…"

Unhampered by this display of civil disobedience, the main focal point of attention was now at the northeast corner of the square. At this location, former governor of the state Jeremiah Morrow took over as official emcee of the proceedings and, in what must have added to the solemnity of the event, a delegation of Freemasons took up post nearby. A massive cornerstone, rough-

Top: No visible markings or dates were placed on the cornerstone when it was put in place in 1839. Capitol Square workers remove a drain pipe from the front of the cornerstone to provide a better view. **Bottom:** The cornerstone is located on the northeast corner of the ground floor of the Ohio Statehouse. A variety of items were packed into the lower stone in 1839, in effect making it a time-capsule. *Photos by Mike Elicson.*

14 THE OHIO STATEHOUSE

ly seven-feet-two inches long by three-feet-three inches deep, had been hewn out of limestone in preparation for the event. An excavation had been made inside the stone for the placement of several items, in effect, making it a time capsule. "The following deposits, securely packed in strong flint glass jars, were packed in an excavation in the lower stone: the Declaration of Independence; the Constitutions of the United States and of the several twenty-six States; the Ordinance of 1787 for the government of the Northwest Territory; the Statutes of Ohio; the Bible; the first two parts of the Transactions of the Historical and Philosophical Society of Ohio; specimens of the gold and silver coins of the United States; one hundred and fifty newspapers of recent date, comprising those published in Ohio and in the chief cities of the Union; several statistical works and periodicals; specimens of Ohio's agricultural and manufacturing productions; reports of the State institutions; the act of the Ohio legislature authorizing the building of the capitol; a list of the officers of the Government of the United States and of the several States, including the judiciary; a list of the members of the last and preceding legislatures of Ohio; the names of the Statehouse commissioners, architect, and superintendent of masonry; as well as a list of the officers of the Corporation of Columbus." (Cummings, ibid, page 39.) Thirteen regular toasts were made that day, including the following which was specific to the cornerstone: "Emblematic of the great State of whose civic temple it is destined to be the support and ornament: Gigantic in its magnitude, impregnable in its strength, enduring in its integrity." (*Regular Toasts*, Columbus, July 4, 1839.) The cornerstone had been held aloft in a harness awaiting its final placement during the ceremony. As it was placed, Jeremiah Morrow stated the following words:

"Let the foundations be deep and strong; let the materials be of nature's most lasting gifts—durable, imperishable; let the edifice rise in solemn, simple grandeur, a monument of chaste and classic beauty. And may the lightnings of Heaven, which scathe, and the whirlwind and storm, which prostrate the works of man, pass by and spare this house, erected by a mighty people, and consecrated to social and constitutional government. And may the councils of truth and justice and public virtue preside in its halls; may discord and faction be put far from them; and may a free and united people, who reared it, and whose temple it is, watch over and cherish within its walls the form and spirit of their republican institutions. And I now lay the cornerstone of the Capitol of Ohio!"

TEMPLE OF DELAY

After this auspicious beginning, the Statehouse project was subjected to a severe delay. The legislation that had created the city of Columbus and made it the state's capitol would expire in 1840, and the same political forces that had urged the relocation of the capitol some two decades earlier again raised their collective heads, putting pressure on the government to move the seat of government once again. By this time, the foundations for the walls of the Statehouse were almost completely finished, rising to ground level—no small feat considering that the massive load-bearing stone blocks that were used for this foundation had been sunk six to ten feet into the ground. The stone, in turn, rested on a prepared gravel bed that had been painstakingly leveled and coated with slurry, a mixture of rock and concrete.

While the question of either moving the capitol city or allowing it to remain in Columbus was simmering, all work on the capitol building ground to a halt. If the government moved its physical location it was obvious that the structure would not be required, so no further effort was expended to complete the place. Open excavations on the site were filled in with earth and the area used as it had been previously, as a public square that accommodated grazing livestock. Columbus was referred to as a *cow town* for many years due to this decision. Although the government, in 1843, decided that Columbus would remain the capitol, three more years would elapse until they felt confident enough to allocate funds and begin work on the nascent Statehouse. When the project initially started up again in 1846, little was accomplished for lack of funds. The most noticeable work was the use of convict labor to unearth the buried foundations and add to them. In their official year end reports for both 1846 and 1847, the commissioners expressed regret at the slow progress that had been made, and blamed that lack of progress on funding.

THE ARCHITECTS

During the twenty-two years it would take to complete the new Ohio Statehouse; five different architects, including Henry Walter who oversaw the foundation work, would lend their expertise to the project. From 1840 to 1848, no architect was employed due to political reasons. Many argued that the state was wast-

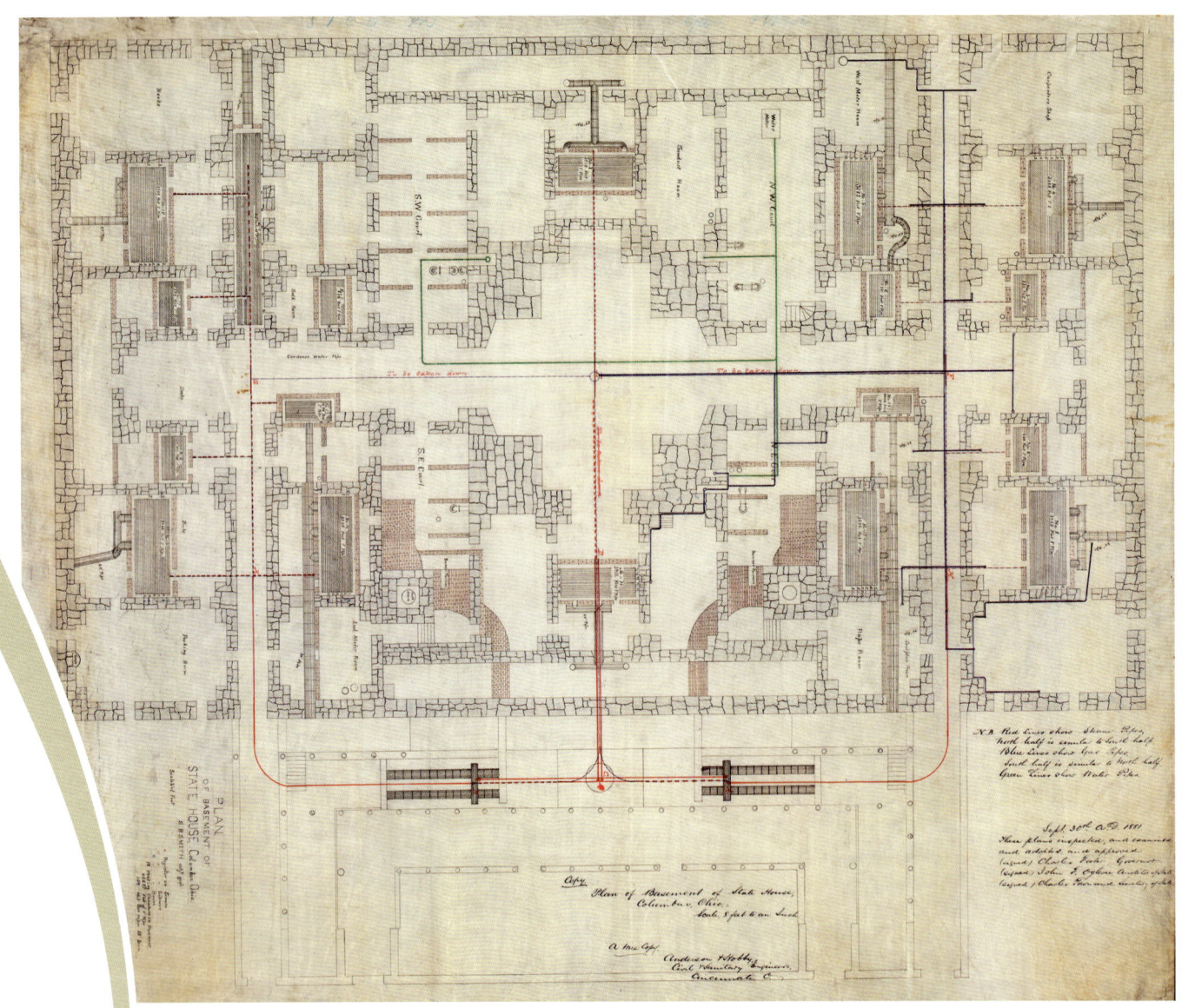

This architectural drawing of the crypt shows its layout in 1881. Besides containing the heating system for the Statehouse, it also housed a packing room, sawdust room, carpenters shop, as well as a sculptor's room. *Courtesy of the Ohio History Connection.*

ing money on a new capitol building that wasn't needed. Describing the Statehouse Square on August 10, 1847, the *Ohio State Journal* mentioned that it was "occupied with shapen and shapeless materials…strewn with promiscuous confusion, and overgrown in many places with rank weeds and thistles." This and other criticisms of the current state of affairs at the capitol helped restore interest and funding of the long neglected project.

The next year would see several noticeable changes, and would be the first year in a string of many that would see great advancement of the Statehouse project. Two Cincinnati men, J.O. Sawyer and William Russell West, were appointed as architects for the building, and with increasing deliveries of stone being delivered to the construction site from the quarry, after a stop at the penitentiary for shaping and finishing, the building achieved a small but verifiable milestone—the sub-basement or Crypt began to peek above the level of the ground. Made almost entirely of brick, the Crypt's barrel arches and vaulted ceilings were in place to receive materials for storage. The Crypt would eventually also house books, a carpenter's shop, and sculptor's room, in addition to being the location of the heating system. Sawyer and West would work on the project from 1848 to 1854, and besides completing the Crypt, they brought the walls of the Statehouse to their present height. Much of the heavy lifting was accomplished by cranes and derricks which reared up above the work site. Stone cutters were hired and worked alongside roughly eighty to one hundred convicts each day. The *Ohio Statesman* reported on June 15, 1853 that, "The stone cutters make the yard ring with the chink of their chisels; the hewn stone moves upward to their places; the oxen and locomotive are busy at work. The boys in stripes (convicts) move pretty briskly for the warm weather. The central columns are rising upward." Indeed, five large derricks were used to pick up the massive stones and place them accordingly and with such speed that the west front of the building was completed that year as well. Controversially, due to disagreements over design with the Statehouse commissioners, West and Sawyer resigned from the project.

In May of 1854, Nathan B. Kelly took over the architect's post and construction began anew. Under his direction the two hundred and fifty ton roof of the capitol,

These two examples of graffiti were left by a former inmate of the State Penitentiary in Columbus. Inmate Ephraim Badger, whose crime was burglary, was incarcerated from 1846 to 1849. He repaid his debt to society in part by toiling on the construction of the crypt in the new Ohio Statehouse. *Top photo by Michael Rupert. Bottom photo by Dan Shellenbarger.*

CORNERSTONE TO CUPOLA 17

THE OLD COLUMBUS STATE HOUSE BURNS TO THE GROUND

February 1, 1852, the old Ohio Statehouse in Columbus is consumed by flames. Newspapers around the country carried the story, like the following in the *New York Times* of February 3, 1852: "Destruction of the Ohio State House. Columbus, Ohio, Sunday, Feb. 1. This morning, about 3¼ o'clock, a fire was discovered in the Senate Chamber of the State House, and the garret and cupola were also found to be in flames. Before the fire could be reached, it burned through the roof of the Senate Chamber, driving out the firemen with the heat and smoke, and the whole chamber was speedily enveloped in flames. Everything was destroyed except the Clerk's desk, which, with his valuable papers, was saved. All the movables in the lower House were also saved. The total loss cannot be estimated. Many old and valuable papers were destroyed. The fire is supposed to have been the work of an incendiary. The Odeon, and the Supreme Court room, will be used by the Legislature until other arrangements are made." The inevitability of a fire had been a concern since the legislative session of 1837-1838, which recognized the danger and authorized the creation of a new capitol building. This was the critical moment which led to a more rapid completion of the new Ohio Statehouse. This article states that the fire was caused by an incendiary. Curiously, the original Ohio Statehouse in Chillicothe, Ohio, also burned to the ground the same year.

made of iron rafters, and covered with wood and copper, was completed. Largely overlooked by all of the previous architects until this point was the interior of the building, and Kelly, a veteran of the Greek Revival movement, was intimately familiar with the chaste and unadorned nature of that school of design. Despite this background, Kelly was responsible for most of the highly decorative and florid elements still seen today inside the Ohio Statehouse.

One of Kelly's other monumental accomplishments was the first heating system put into use at the capitol. Architect Kelly ordered that the interior of the main walls be thoroughly lined with bricks. Pipes or flues were placed between the bricks and the walls to convey steam, which was to heat the building. To generate the steam, four large boilers were placed in the center of the Crypt and these, in turn, were connected by pipes to eighteen air chambers. Essentially, the idea was to heat the air in the air chambers by the system of steam pipes. The heated air would then rise to the different floors of the building venting into each room through flues placed for that purpose. To vent the spent air, two large ventilating stacks, still visible today, were placed on the east side of the building. A steam engine connected to the boilers cycled water to and from two large cisterns (containing 800 barrels of water apiece) placed at the top of the east and west side of the building. They provided water for steam as well as fed several water closets located throughout the maze of floors and rooms. The following winter, the temperature in the partially-built Statehouse rose to a comfortable sixty degrees. (Cummings, ibid, pages 87–91.) During his tenure, gas pipes, fittings, and burners for the same were installed throughout the building to provide lighted rooms and passageways. Elaborate and decorative designs for the House and Senate Chambers, Supreme Courtroom, and Rotunda were carried out by plaster workers, painters, and glazers. Unfortunately, as time went by, Kelly's interior designs and décor were

One of the two large ventilating stacks that were placed, under the direction of architect Nathan Kelly, to vent the spent air of the heating system he designed. In February of 1856, it was reported that the temperature in the House Chambers maintained an even sixty degrees. *Photo by Mike Elicson.*

growing more and more elaborate, rankling critics who were already dissatisfied with the growing costs associated with the new capitol building. Kelly was replaced in 1858 by Isaiah Rogers, the fifth and final architect to oversee and complete the Ohio Statehouse.

Using economy and appearance as his watch-words, architect Rogers began to remove a number of excessive ornaments from the building and to alter any pre-existing plans that called for such. A skylight, twenty-six feet in diameter allowing natural light into the Rotunda, was part of the newly revised plan for the Cupola which sits atop the building. Out of all the design elements of the Ohio Statehouse, the Cupola had undergone the most revisions throughout the construction period. Thomas Cole's original drawing for the Statehouse contest in 1838 had called for a dome, which was rejected by the architect West during his tenure. West had devised a conical roof that was more in keeping with Greek Revival architecture. When Nathan Kelly took over the reins in 1854, he revived Thomas Cole's dome design and added a few flourishes of his own. The final agreed upon design returned the Cupola to the drum shape that West had designed, yet Rogers added a raised skylight that would admit light into the interior. Both the outer Cupola and the interior of the dome-like ceiling of the Rotunda were finished by December of 1859. When workers finally removed the scaffolding from the Rotunda, many were pleased with the overall look. The *Ohio State Journal* for January 3, 1860, states: "The scaffolding that has for years towered in the Rotunda and been such an obstruction and eye-sore of the interior of the State House, has been removed, and now the noble center apartment is the grand attraction of the building. It is the remark of all that a finer specimen of architecture than the Rotunda and interior of the dome does not exist in America. Standing upon the floor, the eye is cast upward one hundred and twenty feet, and rests upon a magnificent skylight of ground and stained glass, the center of which is a beautiful design of the great seal of the State, done in colors most admirably blended; from this radiates a star of red and yellow rays, surrounded with plain ground glass, which, in its turn, is encircled by a belt of rosettes, and the whole is fin-

Left: The access door to the cistern on the third floor, east side, of the Ohio Statehouse is more than halfway up on the wall. The author has just opened the door for a closer look. *Photo by Mike Elicson.* **Below:** Placed high on the east side interior of the Statehouse in 1855, this cistern held eight hundred barrels of water to provide steam for the boilers, as well as feeding several water closets. *Photo by Mike Elicson.*

OHIO STATE CAPITOL FESTIVAL, 1857

Although the new Ohio Statehouse wouldn't be complete until 1861, the construction was far enough along that by January of 1857, the executive, judicial, and legislative branches officially moved into their new quarters. While delivering the governor's annual address that same January, Salmon P. Chase, the first governor to occupy the new Ohio Statehouse, expressed his approval of the work that had been accomplished so far. This included several prominent citizens of Columbus who had started planning a celebration during the previous month. The Capitol Festival as it came to be called was held during the evening of January 6, 1857. "The Capitol during the day had been prepared to accommodate the people; the chairs were removed from the halls of the Senate and House. The rotunda was handsomely decorated with tri-colored muslin and evergreens." (*Ohio Statesmen*, January 14, 1857.) An estimated eight thousand visitors turned out for the event which included food, (including one hundred and twenty-five hams, and one thousand gallons of oysters), speeches, and dancing in the Senate Chamber which lasted until six a.m. the next morning.

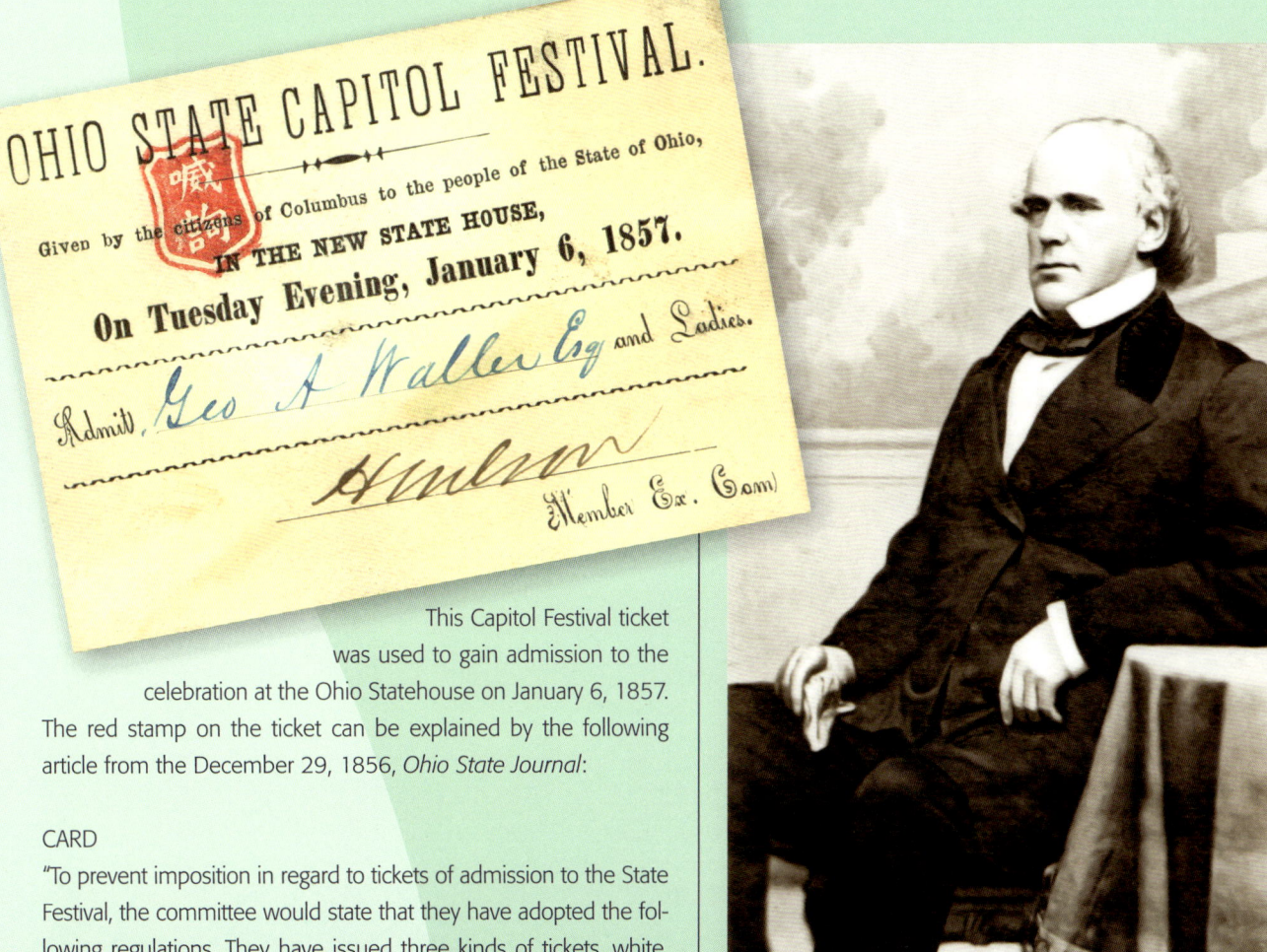

This Capitol Festival ticket was used to gain admission to the celebration at the Ohio Statehouse on January 6, 1857. The red stamp on the ticket can be explained by the following article from the December 29, 1856, *Ohio State Journal*:

CARD
"To prevent imposition in regard to tickets of admission to the State Festival, the committee would state that they have adopted the following regulations. They have issued three kinds of tickets, white, yellow, and red. The white and yellow for the invited guests, will admit all persons residing outside of Franklin county, FREE—and them only. Each resident of Franklin county must present a red ticket at the door. The red tickets can be procured at J.H. Riley & Co., and Randall & Aston's Book Stores, and of Wm. G. Deshler, Treasurer, at five dollars each, admitting one gentleman and ladies." *Museum purchase Capitol Square Review & Advisory Board; 2015.010.001.*

Photograph of Salmon P. Chase, c. 1865–1870. He served two, two year terms as Ohio Governor from 1856–1860. Abraham Lincoln appointed Chase secretary of the treasury on his war-time cabinet and Chief Justice of the United States Supreme Court in 1864. *Courtesy of the Ohio History Connection.*

CORNERSTONE TO CUPOLA

Right: The oldest known photograph of the Ohio Statehouse shows it under construction between 1856 and early 1857. The walls were at their present height, and the copper roof had been completed. The outer brick vault of the cupola was in place, yet only the first floor of windows had been finished. The state offices, (still present in this photo), were torn down in the spring of 1857 preparatory to the grading of the public square. *Courtesy of the Ohio History Connection.* **Below:** A view of Columbus, Ohio, from Capital University, ca. 1860. The almost completed Ohio Statehouse can be seen in the middle background, dominating the city as the tallest building until 1901. This illustration shows how much the city had grown since its creation in 1812. *Courtesy of the Ohio History Connection.*

ished with an outside of plain glass. It makes a pleasing picture; and when the oil paintings, that are ordered, are placed in the panels, the Rotunda of the Ohio State House will vie in magnificence with similar buildings of the world."

Now that the scaffolding had been removed, plans moved forward to complete the Rotunda in its entirety. The June 27, 1860 issue of the *Ohio State Journal* mentioned: "Workmen are engaged in the Rotunda of the State House, preparing to lay down a marble floor, of great permanence and beautiful appearance." The work was done with four different kinds of marble—Italian white, Lisbon red-yellow, American black, and green slate. The workmen began laying the octagon shaped tiles in the center of the floor with a star design, and gradually worked their way outward placing four thousand nine hundred and fifty seven pieces. One of the most unique floors in any of America's public buildings to this day, the Rotunda floor was complete in October of the same year. The grounds of the Statehouse had been receiving attention, as well, now that the yard was no longer being used as a place of storage for stone and steam engines.

Winding walkways were being constructed as well as trees and shrubbery were planted in such a fashion as to not block the view of the newly finished building. A decorative iron fence had been placed around the square and an article in the November 21, 1860, *Ohio State Journal* reported: "The iron fence enclosing the State House grounds is being painted by Mr. Francis Harris, with a new kind of paint called "Milk's Patent Rubber Paint." It is a composition of coal tar, india rubber, and some other ingredients, and makes a beautiful shining black, and is prepared by Messrs. Armstrong & Jones, of this city. It is said to be an excellent preparation for iron which is exposed to the weather, keeping it entirely free from rust." Statehouse Superintendent William Platt reported that same month that the building of the Ohio Statehouse is now complete. In truth, it would almost be another full year before the final door was hung and the last bit of plastering was completed. The final price tag for the twenty-two year construction was $1,359,121.45, stated in a report from November 15, 1861. No celebration was planned or held to mark the occasion of completing the building. Looming large in the background during the final days of construction of the Ohio Statehouse and now taking center stage in the minds of the people of Ohio and the United States, was the momentous issue of the American Civil War.

DIMENSIONS OF THE OHIO STATEHOUSE

When completed in 1861, the Ohio Statehouse was the second largest building in the nation (the U.S. Capitol being the largest). The following list provides the dimensions of the Statehouse shortly after its completion. This list was found in the *Report of the Superintendent of the Statehouse, 1863*.

EXTERIOR

The Capitol presents four fronts, with colonnades, and is 184 feet wide by 304 feet long.

The East and West steps are 20½ feet wide and 117 feet long.

The North and South steps are 20½ feet wide and 57 feet long.

The Broad Terrace, from the East Portico is 73 feet wide by 209½ feet long.

The Terrace on all other sides of the house is 18 feet wide.

The Portico on the West front is 15 feet 4 inches deep by 122 feet long.

The Portico on the East front is 15 feet 4 inches deep by 120 feet long.

The Porticos on the North and South sides are each 14 feet 4 inches deep by 57½ feet long.

Eight Columns on the East and West fronts are each 6 feet 2 inches base diameter and 36 feet high.

Four Columns on the North and South fronts are each 6 feet 2 inches.

Area of the building, including terrace and steps, a little over 2 acres.

Height of the building from the ground to the top of the blocking course, 61 feet.

Height of the building from the ground to the top of the pinnacle of Cupola, 158 feet.

INTERIOR

The chief entrance is from the West.

Height of the Terrace from the ground, 5 feet.

Height of the Portico from the ground, 9 feet, 8 inches.

Height of the Rotunda floor from the ground, 16 feet, 6 inches.

Height of the House of Representatives and Senate floor from ground, 30 feet.

Height of the stone arches above Rotunda floor, 36 feet, 8 inches.

Diameter of the Rotunda floor, 64 feet, 5 inches.

Diameter of the Cupola (outside), 75 feet.

Width of the main corridors in the building, 23 feet, 5 inches.

The Ohio Statehouse, circa 1861. *Courtesy of the Ohio History Connection.*

Width of the cross corridors in the building, 9 feet, 4 inches.
(THE STATE HOUSE, from the *Report of the Superintendent of the Statehouse, 1863.*)

LINCOLN

In September of 1859, Abraham Lincoln spoke to a group of about one hundred who had gathered in front of the east terrace of the Ohio Statehouse. This was after the famous Lincoln-Douglas debates in which Lincoln, the republican candidate for the U.S. Senate from Illinois, lost the election to the incumbent democratic senator, Stephen Douglas. These debates had caught the attention and imagination of the people, and when Lincoln spoke at the Ohio Statehouse on September 16, 1859, it was in support of the republican candidate for governor of Ohio that year, William Dennison. Political maps of Ohio at this time showed the state to be largely democratic, yet despite this, William Dennison did indeed win the election and became Ohio's first republican governor.

Abraham Lincoln went on to win the presidential election of 1860. On February 13, 1861 a Grand

Ovation to the President-Elect took place at the Ohio Statehouse. Lincoln, who was on his way to Washington, DC, to be officially sworn in as President was stopping at a number of locations along the way. He was officially greeted by Governor Dennison, the legislature, and reportedly over five thousand citizens who had turned out for the occasion. The President-elect spoke in the House Chamber to a joint session (both Senate and House members) of the legislature, at the close of which the applause, according to the *Ohio State Journal* of February 14, 1861, was quick and hearty. The same article reported that at half-past eight o'clock that same night a Monster Levee was held at the capitol, where the President-elect met "many of our citizens, and exchanging with them pleasant salutations." By the time Abraham Lincoln was sworn in as sixteenth President of the United States, (March 4, 1861), seven southern states had already seceded from the Union. During the years of the American Civil War, Union soldiers from Ohio were billeted from time-to-time at the Statehouse. Some reports noted that the soldiers slept in the Rotunda and received pen and paper from legislators to write home to their loved ones. For four long years the war raged between north and south.

Abraham Lincoln would make one final visit to the Ohio Statehouse. On April 29, 1865, the funeral train carrying the fallen president made an official stop in Columbus. The coffin was placed in a funeral hearse, driven to the Statehouse, and placed upon a catafalque in the center of the Rotunda. The body rested there for eight hours, and it has been estimated that fifty thousand Ohioans turned out that day to pay their respects to the former president.

This plaque marks the location of Abraham Lincoln's first visit to the Ohio Statehouse. *Photo by Mike Elicson.*

Left: The Presidential Journey—Reception of the President In The Hall of the Legislature of Columbus, Ohio—The Senate and Legislature In Joint Session. From a sketch by our Special Artist traveling in the Presidential Train. *Frank Leslie's Illustrated Newspaper, March 2, 1861.* **Right:** Portrait of William Dennison, Governor of Ohio: 1860–1862, by John Henry Witt. Abraham Lincoln campaigned on Dennison's behalf at the Ohio Statehouse in 1859. *Garth's Auctioneers & Appraisers, Delaware, Ohio.*

Top left: With the flags flying at half-mast on Capitol Square, the 88th Ohio Volunteer Infantry escorts the fallen president on April 29, 1865. *Courtesy of the Ohio History Connection.* **Top right:** Carte de visite of Abraham Lincoln's catafalque in the Ohio Statehouse Rotunda, April 29, 1865. *Courtesy of the Ohio History Connection.* **Center:** It was reported that fifty thousand mourners turned out to pay their respects during the eight hours that Lincoln's body lay in repose. This photograph shows the Ohio Statehouse columns and windows draped in black crepe. A sign above the entrance reads, "With Malice to No One, With Charity For All." *Courtesy of the Ohio History Connection.* **Bottom left:** Abraham Lincoln's body laid in repose for eight hours in the Rotunda of the Ohio Statehouse. In this image, Lincoln's funeral hearse is empty, awaiting the return of his remains, before continuing the journey to Springfield, Illinois. *Courtesy of the Ohio History Connection.*

CORNERSTONE TO CUPOLA

The Architect of the Capitol, Robert D. Loversidge, who led most of the renovation work on the Ohio Statehouse, had this to say about the wood carving in the Capitol building: "I think the carving on the second floor of the Statehouse is special. The work in the House and Senate Chambers, and doorways to the Supreme Court (Speaker's Office today) is really great, especially now that we have removed half an inch of paint, and replaced it with graining. I especially admire the House windows, under the gallery, where the carved wood blends seamlessly into the embedded cast iron brackets that hold up the gallery." (Loversidge, Robert D., response to an inquiry from the author regarding the carved woodwork in the Statehouse, January 18, 2017.) *Photos by Michael Rupert.*

ENGLISH JOHN

During the twenty-two year construction of the Ohio Statehouse, (1839-1861); numerous artists, craftsmen, and skilled laborers, lent their talent to creating our magnificent state capitol building. And although we know the names of the architects, superintendents, and Statehouse commissioners who worked on the project, we know very little about the individual craftsmen whose work can still be seen today. The following article came from the descendants of John Robinson, who was born in London, England, on March 21, 1802. He received a liberal education and in his early youth learned the woodcarvers business. In 1833, John and his wife sailed for America to begin a new life. They eventually settled in Union County, Ohio, and made it their permanent home. According to their family history, Mr. Robinson was a man of broad scholarly attainments and superior scientific knowledge. He collected and classified the fungi of Ohio, making accurate drawings of the same. Yet he was also known as a skilled woodcarver and much of his work, according to the family history, could be seen at the Statehouse in Columbus.

REMOVAL OF LIBRARY WALNUT RECALLS ARTISTRY

"Removal of the hand-carved black walnut finishings from the old quarters of the state library in the Capitol Building has been effected with little regard, probably in complete ignorance that the work on them is supposed to have been done by a man who held the reputation of being, at the time, the foremost woodcarver in the United States. He is credited with having done the artistic work on the walnut decorations that once attracted attention in the Senate Chamber and certainly was the artist who put his talents into the making of a beautiful walnut mantle piece that mysteriously disappeared from the library a few years ago. The artist was an eccentric Englishman who lived for many years on a farm in Union County on the Delaware County line—John Robinson, familiarly known among his neighbors, but not to his face, for he was a man who stood on dignity, as 'English John.'" (Excerpt from the *Columbus Dispatch*, July 22, 1934. By George H. Gordon.)

This wood carving above the door leading to the Speaker of the Ohio House of Representatives office may be the work of John (English John) Robinson. *Photo by Michael Rupert.*

CORNERSTONE TO CUPOLA 29

DECLINE AND RENOVATION

Since 1861, the Ohio Statehouse has maintained its position as both the seat of state government as well as a symbol of our democratic heritage. For over one hundred and fifty years, countless Ohioans have passed through its halls and marveled at its monumental architecture. Civil discourse and debate have echoed throughout its hearing rooms and chambers, to make Ohio a better place for its residents. By the 1980s, the outer appearance of the Statehouse had changed little since its completion in the latter half of the nineteenth century. Within its limestone walls, however, many changes had taken place.

When it was originally completed in 1861, the Ohio Statehouse contained fifty-three rooms that housed all three branches of government on three floors. Yet good and proper government grew to meet the needs of the people, and by 1988 the once spacious interior of the Ohio Statehouse had been transformed into a labyrinth of three hundred and seventeen rooms, with as many as nine floors! Rooms and hallways had been divided up and new offices and meeting spaces created. Years

Towering cranes dominated downtown Columbus and Capitol Square during the renovation. *Photos by Dan Shellenbarger.*

An overhead shot showing the roof of the Ohio Statehouse during the renovation. The original roof weighed two hundred and fifty tons, and was made out of wood with iron rafters and a copper top. At the completion of the renovation, the roof of the Ohio Statehouse was again sheathed in copper. *Photo by Dan Shellenbarger.*

would pass, and then those spaces would be divided up again. Electrical work wasn't always kept current and in some cases wasn't able to run modern office equipment, leaving exposed wiring that had been hastily added to fix the problems. The beautiful, hand-carved woodwork in the Senate and House Chambers, and throughout the Statehouse for that matter, had been covered over with countless coats of paint. No sprinkler system had ever been installed, recalling earlier fears of fire that led to the creation of the new Statehouse in the first place. At times, various office holders would find new cracks in the ceilings when they returned to work in the morning, along with dirt and debris on their desks. It became increasingly apparent that the Ohio Statehouse needed some special attention before it literally crumbled to the ground. That same year, a request for a massive renovation of Capitol Square and the Ohio Statehouse was spearheaded by former Senator Richard H. Finan of Cincinnati, Ohio. Finan persuaded former legislators and governors to partner with him and other outside organizations to get behind the idea of restoring the capitol. In consideration of this idea, the state commissioned Schooley

CORNERSTONE TO CUPOLA 31

Caldwell and Associates to create a master plan for renovation, and in 1989 it was completed. The Capitol Square Renovation Foundation formed that year as well to solicit private donors to get involved in the project, raising more than 10 million dollars. Renovation work began initially on the Senate Building, which was completed in 1992. While this work was being done, a stone connector or Atrium was added, linking the Senate Building to the Statehouse. To further facilitate the renovation, the House of Representatives moved their office space to the Vern Riffe State Office Tower, directly across the street. The Senate moved into the Senate Building on Capitol Square, and held their sessions in the old Supreme Court library. The executive branch relocated as well, taking up a floor of offices in the Riffe Tower. Just as it had been when the new Ohio Statehouse was first constructed, a fence was placed around Capitol Square.

Construction crews labored at dismantling old offices, removing paint, and revealing original marble floors. Towering cranes dominated the square, giving downtown workers a curious view, while the heavy lifting was completed. Electricians completely updated the wiring; stone masons repaired and or replaced crumbling limestone, granite, and marble. Several layers of paint were removed from the walls of the Rotunda, as well as the woodwork of the Senate and House Chambers, which was replaced with graining. Two full years of reconstruction were required to return the Ohio Statehouse to its original grandeur. It was completed in 1996, ready to welcome back the 121st Ohio General Assembly.

WITHIN THE WALLS

The Ohio Statehouse is not a copy of any pre-existing Greek temple from antiquity. It is however, built in the understated and uncomplicated Greek Revival style popular in America at the time of its construction. This style, which harkened back to ancient Greece—the first democracy in the western world,— became the first truly national style architecture in our country's early years. Architect Frank Lloyd Wright rightly proclaimed the Ohio Statehouse to be, "the most honest of all American Statehouses."

Today, within the limestone walls of the Ohio Statehouse are the chambers and hearing rooms of the Ohio General Assembly, the office of the governor, as well as the ceremonial offices of the treasurer and auditor of state. Other tenants located inside are the Legislative Services Commission Bill Room, Press and Broadcast

These objects and many others were found within the walls of the Ohio Statehouse during the renovation. The objects are: (top to bottom) A shoe box bearing a label, (The label reads: *The Excelsior Shoe Company Fine Shoes. Portsmouth, Ohio*) containing the remains of a cat, a rosary, a penknife, and a gaslight fixture or Escutcheon, which was used to disguise the rough openings where gas pipes entered a room. *Found in Collections; Capitol Square Review & Advisory Board. Photo by Michael Rupert.*

32 THE OHIO STATEHOUSE

News Rooms, Capitol Café, as well as Ohio Government Telecommunications which comes complete with a full-fledged studio. Also head quartered at the capitol are the offices of the Capitol Square Review & Advisory Board who are responsible for maintaining the historic character of the Statehouse and Capitol Square while providing for the health, safety, and convenience of those who work in, or visit the complex.

THE ROTUNDA

Symbolism clearly played a role in the decision to build the Ohio Statehouse in the Greek Revival style, as is evidenced in the speechmaking from its first ceremonial occasion: the laying of the cornerstone. Consider that when the Ohio Statehouse was first complete in 1861, it held all three branches of government, and in the midst of these three branches, a noble center apartment—the Rotunda. The Rotunda is also known as the *People's Room*, which is in turn bathed in sunlight from the Cupola, above, symbolically giving light to the voice of the people. Throughout the years, the Rotunda has been a crossroads as well as a gathering place at the capitol for visitors, lobbyists, and politicians. It has been the site of celebrations, such as governor's inaugural ceremonies, and mourning, as when Ohio astronaut and Senator John H. Glenn, Jr. laid in repose in 2016. The Rotunda is the most symbolic room in the Ohio Statehouse, and a sense of reverence for Ohio and its history is felt within its walls.

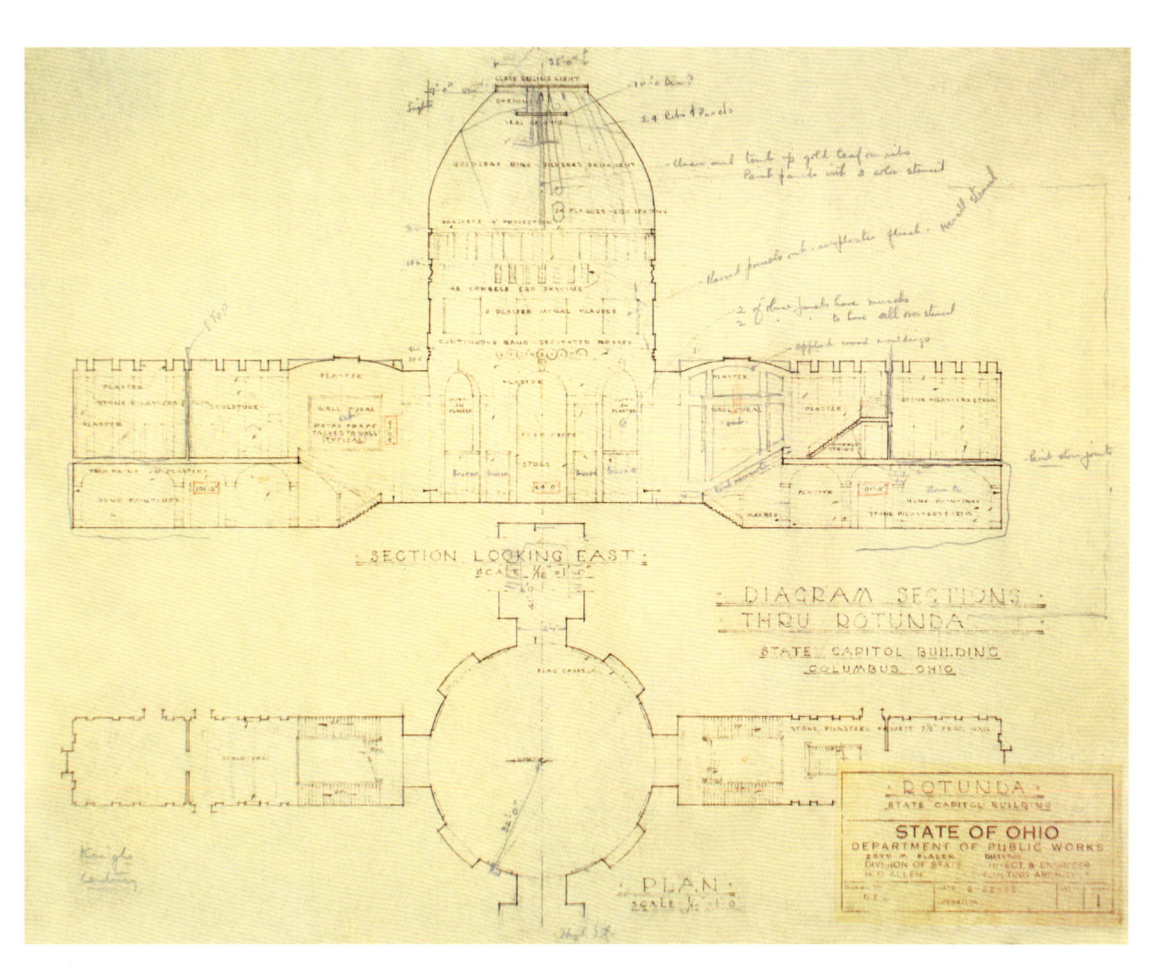

This 1955 State of Ohio Department of Public Works drawing of the Rotunda shows the location of wall murals and sculpture, as well as the location of Ohio's regimental battle flags from the American Civil War. In 1965, the flags were removed from display and were stored in the Judiciary Annex until 1971, when they were officially transferred to the Ohio Historical Society for museum conservation. *Courtesy of former Speaker of the Ohio House of Representatives, William G. Batchelder III.*

The view of the Rotunda entering from the east side of the Statehouse. *Photo by Mike Elicson.*

34 THE OHIO STATEHOUSE

Left: The skylight bathes the interior of the Rotunda with sunlight. *Photo by Richard W. Burry.*

Right: A close up view of the skylight in the Rotunda. The central design is a hand-painted reproduction of the 1847 Great Seal of Ohio. *Photo by Mike Elicson.*

Above: Completed in October of 1860, the Rotunda floor has four thousand nine hundred and fifty-seven pieces of tile. Here, U.S. Marines stand guard during the repose of Ohio astronaut and Senator John H. Glenn, Jr., December 16, 2016. *Photo by Mike Elicson.* **Right:** The Rotunda draped in black in observance of the funeral of President William McKinley, September 19, 1901. *Courtesy of the Ohio History Connection.*

ARTWORK OF THE ROTUNDA

The Signing of the Treaty of Greene Ville

Prior to the signing of the Treaty of Greene Ville, two different American armies had marched into the Ohio Country to wrest control of the territory from the Native American tribes living here. These armies had been led by General Josiah Harmar and General Arthur St. Clair, in 1790 and 1791 respectively. Both of these battle campaigns were complete failures, with the U.S. troops being defeated handily by several different tribes combined under the leadership of Mishikinikwa, or Little Turtle. In 1794, a third American army under the command of General "Mad" Anthony Wayne defeated this Native American confederacy at the Battle of Fallen Timbers. This battle, which took place near present day Toledo, Ohio, resulted in the signing of the Treaty of Greene Ville in 1795. The Treaty of Greene Ville allowed settlement of the Ohio Country up to the treaty line near the Great Black Swamp, (present day Toledo). Little Turtle, standing on the left with arms raised holding a wampum belt, represents the Native Americans at the treaty signing. General Wayne stands on the right side with his officers, while William Wells, an interpreter, stands between both groups. This treaty is considered a fundamental document in the formation of the State of Ohio.

Title: The Signing of the Treaty of Greene Ville. **Artist:** Howard Chandler Christy (1873–1952), Ohio. **Dates:** Commissioned January 1945; unveiled August 1945. **Media:** Oil on canvas attached to board. **Size:** 22 feet by 17 feet. *Photo by Dan Shellenbarger.*

Title: Perry's Victory. **Artist:** William Henry Powell (1823–1879), Ohio. **Dates:** Commissioned 1857; exhibited 1865. **Media:** Oil on canvas. **Size:** 14 feet by 18 feet. *Photo by Dan Shellenbarger.*

Perry's Victory

Largely forgotten today, the Battle of Lake Erie on September 10, 1813, was a turning point in the War of 1812. This battle, which pitted the U.S. fleet under the command of Commodore Oliver Hazard Perry, against a British Royal Naval Squadron commanded by Captain Robert Barclay, was celebrated as a major American victory until the time of the American Civil War. For approximately two-and-a-half hours, Perry's flagship the U.S.S. Lawrence took a severe pounding during the battle; her cannons almost completely silenced. This painting captures the moment when Commodore Perry was rowed to another American vessel, the U.S.S. Niagara, through a half mile of heavy gunfire. Once aboard, he took command, and in short order turned the tide on the Royal Navy Squadron, capturing every ship. Perry's victory on Lake Erie directly resulted in the British evacuation of America, their forces retreating into Canada.

Dawn of a New Light

Thomas Alva Edison (1847–1931), born in Milan, Ohio, has been described as America's greatest inventor. His inventions which include the phonograph, motion picture camera, the light bulb, and many others, continue to influence daily life in the world to this day. For his truly innovative work, Thomas Edison received

Title: Dawn of a New Light. **Artist:** Howard Chandler Christy (1873–1952), Ohio. **Dates:** Installed 1950; went to storage 1964; installed 2001. **Media:** Oil on canvas. **Size:** 9 feet by 12 feet. *Photo by Dan Shellenbarger.*

Title: Orville and Wilbur Wright and Their Accomplishments. **Artist:** Dwight Mutchler (1903–1976), Athens, Ohio. **Dates:** Commissioned 1957; unveiled 1959; put in storage 1964; reinstalled 2004. **Size:** 9 feet by 12 feet. *Photo by Dan Shellenbarger.*

many awards. Describing his work, Edison is quoted as saying: "Genius is one percent inspiration and ninety-nine percent perspiration." This painting shows Edison in three stages of his life: as a youth selling newspapers; as a middle-aged inventor; and as an older man with over one thousand patents. In celebration of perhaps his greatest invention, the incandescent electric light bulb, the French government presented Edison with a statue, *The Spirit of Life*, which can be seen in the upper left of the painting.

Wilbur and Orville Wright and Their Accomplishments
Orville and Wilbur, the Wright brothers, are credited with inventing, building, and flying the world's first successful airplane. Originally from Dayton, Ohio, the brothers gained mechanical skills while working with motors and printing presses and also running a bicycle shop. They moved their operation to Kitty Hawk, North Carolina, where they made the first controlled, sustained flight of a powered, heavier-than-air aircraft on December 17, 1903. This painting illustrates their Dayton, Ohio, home and bicycle shop as well as the site of their historic flight in Kitty Hawk, North Carolina.

Lincoln and Soldiers' Monument
The Lincoln and Soldiers' Monument was presented to the state of Ohio by the Ohio Monument Association in 1871. The massive marble and granite monument was sculpted by Thomas Dow Jones of Granville, Ohio, and is placed in a niche in the Rotunda. The monument consists of a bust of Abraham Lincoln, and a carved central panel that depicts the Confederate Army officers surrendering

This detail of the carved central panel shows victorious Union General Ulysses S. Grant accepting the surrender of Confederate General John C. Pemberton, at the conclusion of the Battle of Vicksburg on July 4, 1863. *Photo by Mike Elicson.*

Title: Lincoln and Soldiers' Monument. **Artist:** T.D. Jones (1811–1881), Granville, Ohio. **Dates:** Commissioned 1865; unveiled 1871. **Media:** Carrara marble (white) and Quincy granite (black). **Size:** 14 feet by 7 feet by 4 feet. **Weight:** Approximately 10,000 pounds.
Photo by Mike Elicson. Inset photo below by Dan Shellenbarger.

BOWEN. MONTGOMERY. PEMBERTON. GRANT. McPHERSON. SHERMAN.
VICKSBURG JULY 4, 1863

"CARE FOR HIM WHO SHALL HAVE BORNE THE BATTLE, AND FOR HIS WIDOW AND HIS ORPHANS."

LINCOLN

to the victorious Union Army officers, after the Battle of Vicksburg on July 4, 1863. Above the base is a quote from Lincoln's second presidential inaugural address, "Care for him who shall have borne the battle and for his widow and his orphans." Responding positively to the unveiling of the Lincoln and Soldiers' Monument, the *Ohio State Journal* of January 21, 1871, stated: "We hope to live to see the day when the approaches to our noble Capitol will be lined with the statues of our greatest statesmen and most heroic men, whose images will daily remind us of the noble lives they lived and whose virtues and example will lead others up the immortal way."

William "Billy" Addison Ireland (1880–1935) was a cartoonist who worked for the *Columbus Dispatch*, and drew editorial cartoons and spot illustrations. This circa 1910–1915 cartoon is a clipping from a larger weekly editorial cartoon called *The Passing Show*, which was a commentary on current events. Describing himself as the janitor of *The Passing Show*, Ireland drew himself into his cartoons and can be seen in this rendering of a busy day in the Rotunda of the Ohio Statehouse. *Found in Collections; Capitol Square Review & Advisory Board.*

Photo by Mike Elicson.

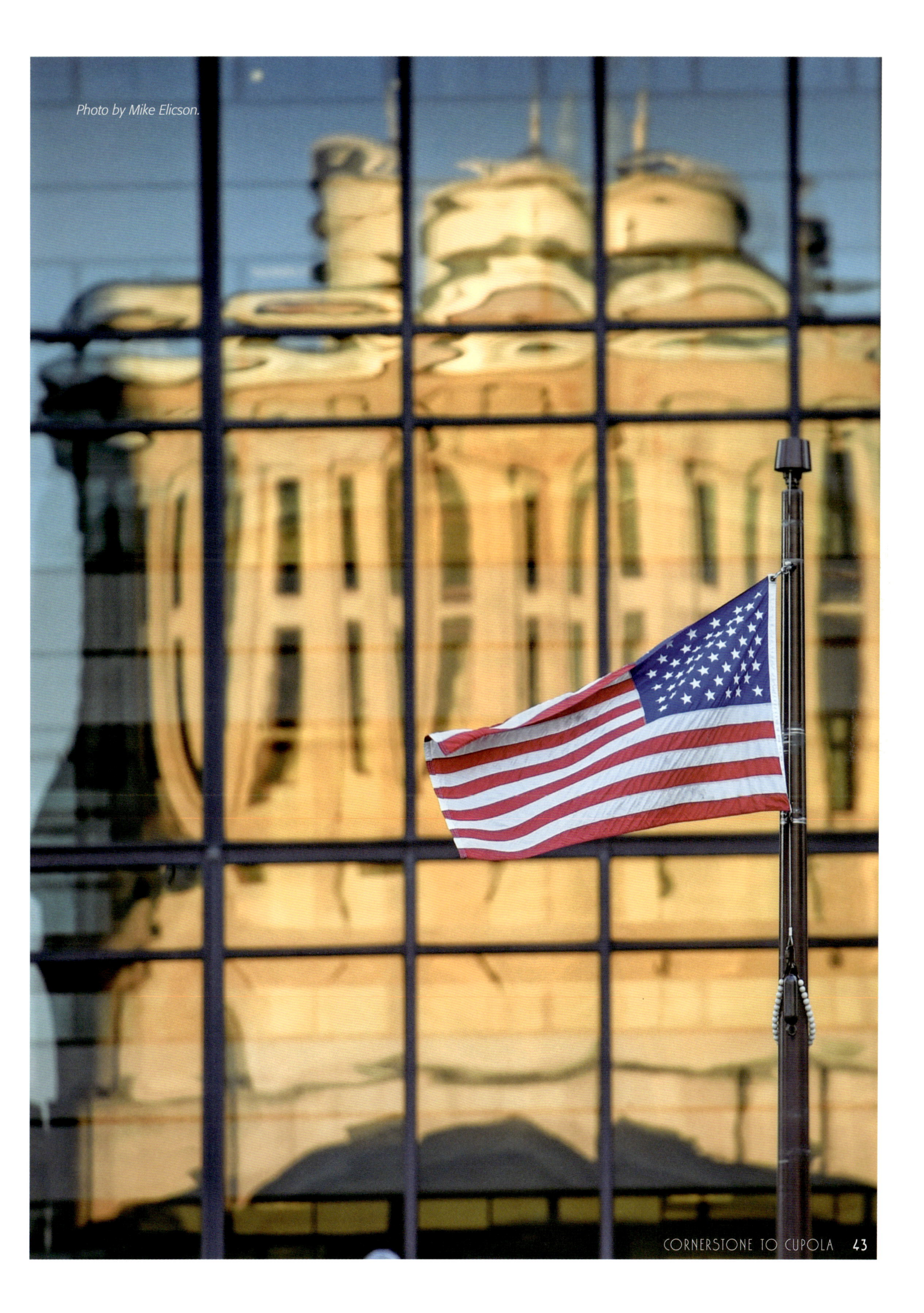

THE CUPOLA

The Cupola of the Ohio Statehouse stands out as unique among her sister state capitol buildings. Its design was constantly being challenged and changed throughout the twenty-two year construction span. It was the decision of the final architect, Isaiah Rogers, to return to a Cupola, rather than a dome, which gives the Ohio Statehouse that understated elegance that is typical of Greek Revival architecture. The Cupola is one of the most curious and distinctive features of the Statehouse to this day, contributing to one of the most asked questions from visitors: "Where is your dome?"

Photo by Mike Elicson.

CORNERSTONE TO CUPOLA 45

After ascending three floors of a spiraling Ohio limestone staircase, the walls close in to approximately twenty-four inches across, allowing only one person at a time to climb these narrow stairs to the first floor of windows in the Cupola. To gain access to the observation deck from the first floor of windows, travelers must climb a final set of twenty wooden stairs. *Photo by Mike Elicson.*

The glass and steel oculus of the raised skylight of the Cupola was the design idea that Isaiah Rogers used to cap the Capitol. *Photo by Mike Elicson.*

CORNERSTONE TO CUPOLA 47

The observation deck or observation gallery was a popular destination for visitors travelling to Columbus to visit the Ohio Statehouse. *Photos by Mike Elicson.*

48 THE OHIO STATEHOUSE

OFF LIMITS!

The Ohio limestone spiral staircase that is accessible from the Crypt or ground floor twists and turns its way upwards through the floors of the Ohio Statehouse, terminating at the first floor of windows in the Cupola that leads to the wooden staircase. Today, these staircases and the observation deck of the Cupola are off limits, and require special permission to gain access. The off-limits status is largely due to liability reasons, as well as museum conservation. This rule went into effect in the early twentieth century; the need for which is evidenced in the following newspaper article from the *Ohio State Journal*, April 24, 1921:

NO MORE VIEWS OF CITY FROM CAPITOL DOME

"Remember the time you climbed the long, narrow, rickety, wood stairway to the Statehouse dome to get a birdseye view of the city? You don't recall having done so the last half dozen years, for no one has—except employees on business. Chances are the dome will never again be open to the public, according to Adjutant General Florence. Too frequently, timid folks got dizzy and came near collapsing when coming to the top of the unbanistered, ramshackle stairway. True, the stairs might be rebuilt and rendered safe to climbers, but, the real objection, at least one which cannot be remedied so easily, is that there is only one entrance to and exit from the dome. It is so narrow as to permit only one person at a time to pass through it. Florence believes it would be next to unlawful, if not entirely so, under the circumstances, to permit the public to use the dome for sightseeing purposes."

The long, narrow, rickety, wood stairway, that leads to the observation deck of the Cupola today. *Photo by Mike Elicson.*

Photo by Mike Elicson.

OHIO GENERAL ASSEMBLY

Since 1857, when the Ohio Statehouse was far enough along in construction, the Ohio General Assembly has filled the halls and pursued the business of government. Each citizen of the state is represented by a state representative and a state senator. There are one hundred and thirty-two members of the Ohio General Assembly, with the state divided into ninety-nine house districts, and thirty-three senate districts. Members of the house and senate are assigned to standing committees and hear testimony from interested citizens participating in the legislative process. During floor sessions in the House and Senate Chambers, members debate the merits of a proposal, and then cast their vote for or against the bill. Legislators in the Ohio House vote electronically with the results tallied on two screens on each side of the chamber. Senators vote traditionally, that is, they approve or reject legislation verbally in a roll call style vote. Legislative desks in the House and Senate Chambers are reproduced in the style of the originals, yet have been modified for 21st century government. The marble desks used by the Speaker of the House and the Senate President are original. During the renovation of the Statehouse, several coats of paint were removed from the walls and woodwork of the chambers. The paint colors today are reproductions of the originals.

50 THE OHIO STATEHOUSE

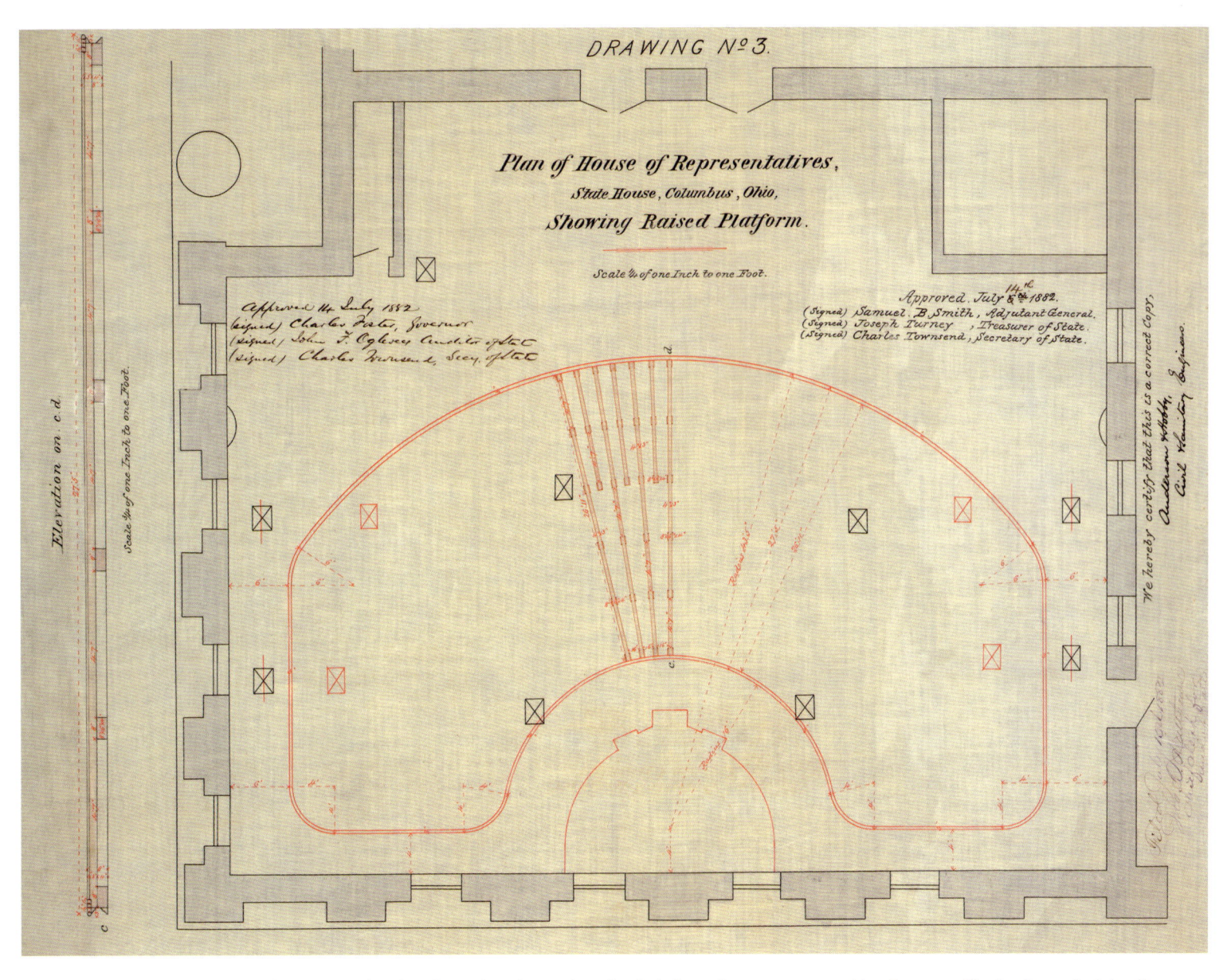

This original drawing of the House Chamber floor plan shows the raised platform that was approved by Governor Charles Foster in July of 1882. *Courtesy of the Ohio History Connection.*

HOUSE CHAMBER

It has already been noted that architect Nathan Kelly was mainly responsible for the highly decorative and florid elements still seen today within the Statehouse. His elaborate ornamental details earned the wrath of the Statehouse Commissioners who felt that they were not in character with the style of the building. Although many of his design elements were eventually removed, and Kelly dismissed from the project, the House Chamber is still the best example of his decorative work.

This view of the floor of the renovated House Chamber shows the raised platform, originally designed in 1882, still in use today. *Photo by Michael Rupert.*

CORNERSTONE TO CUPOLA 51

Below: In 1857, when the legislators first occupied the House and Senate Chambers, they began to complain that there wasn't enough light. In the 1870s, additional windows were added to correct this problem. This 1876 drawing shows the details of the ceiling lights or windows, and was approved by Governor Rutherford B. Hayes. *Courtesy of the Ohio History Connection.* **Bottom:** The ornate ceiling lights admit sunlight into the House Chamber; symbolically providing illumination and enlightenment to the legislators who are working on behalf of the people. *Photo by Michael Rupert.*

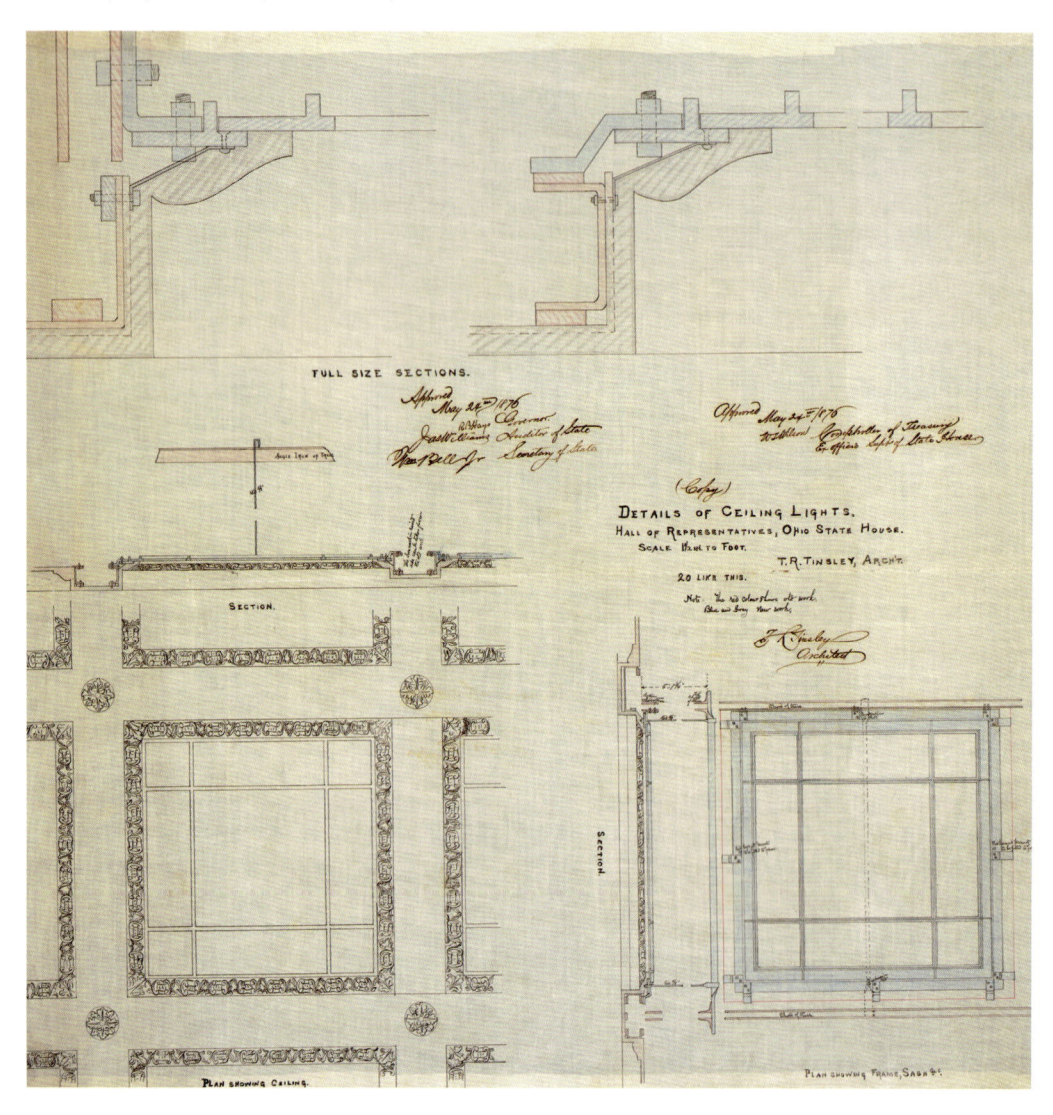

52 THE OHIO STATEHOUSE

Above and left: As called for in the 1876 re-fit of the windows in the House Chamber, the ceiling today has twenty windows, or ceiling lights. *Photos by Mike Elicson.*

Above: All of the electric lighting in the Ohio Statehouse today has been made to look like the original gas lights-complete with knobs to turn on and off the gas. *Photos by Mike Elicson.* **Right:** Visitors may watch the proceedings on the floor of the House Chamber from the public balcony galleries, located on three sides of the chamber. *Photo by Mike Elicson.*

54 THE OHIO STATEHOUSE

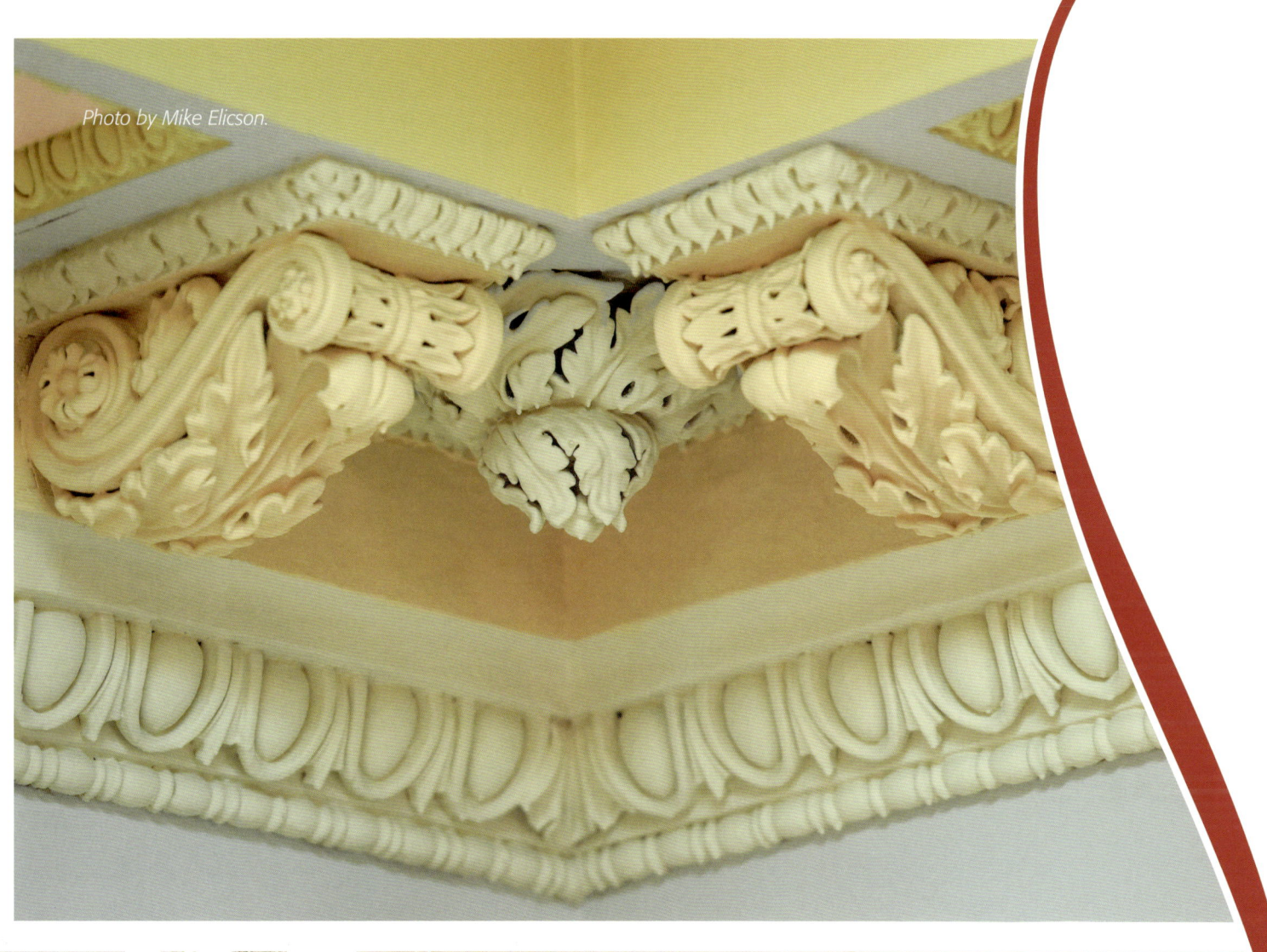

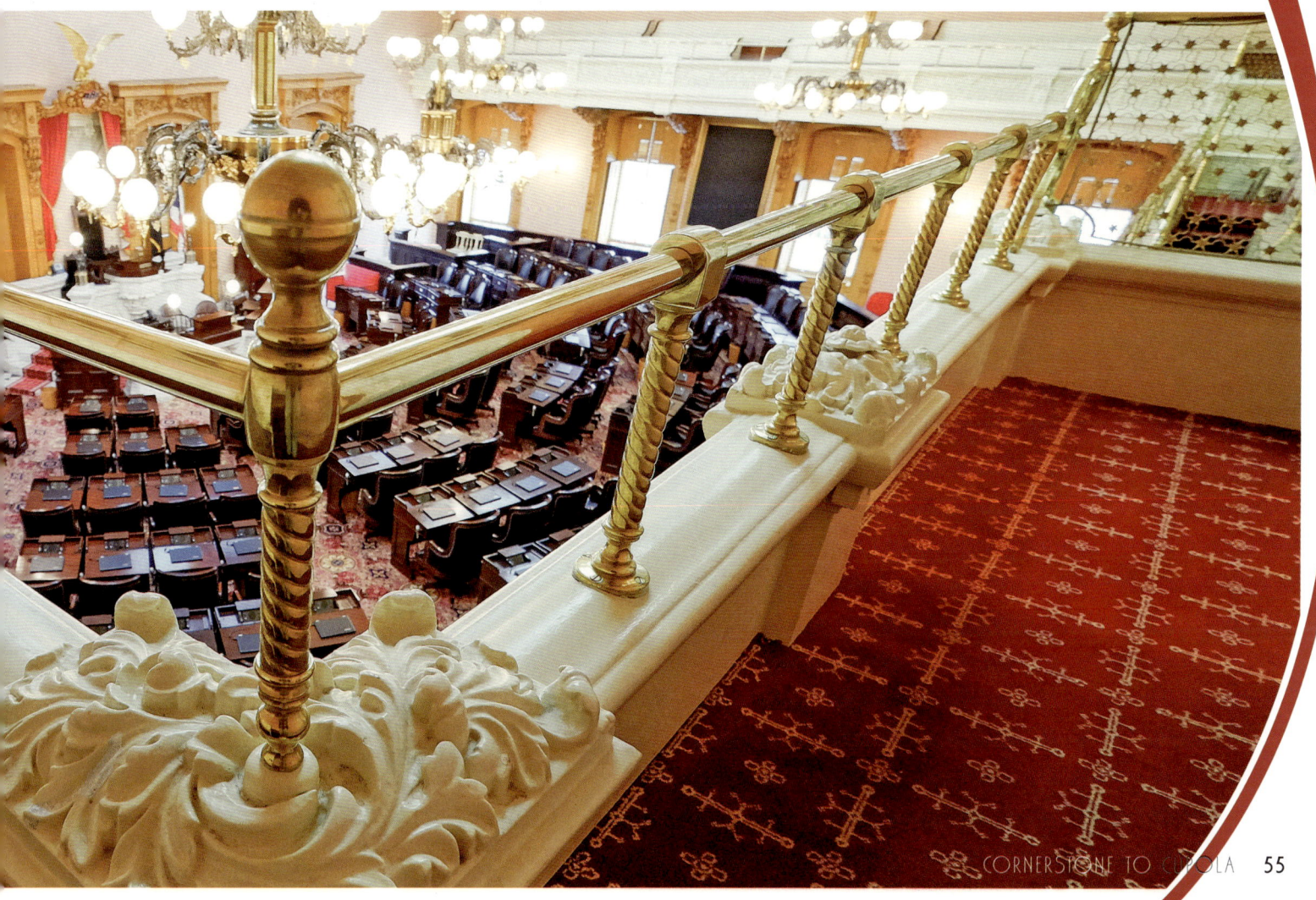

Photo by Mike Elicson.

CORNERSTONE TO CUPOLA 55

Architect Nathan Kelly, who worked on the Statehouse project from 1854–1858, is responsible for most of the florid detailing of the interior of the Capitol; including this column in the House Chamber. *Photos by Mike Elicson.*

56 THE OHIO STATEHOUSE

CORNERSTONE TO CUPOLA 57

Right: This September 1855 drawing by architect Nathan Kelly shows some of the *florid* detailing added to the massive Speaker's desk. *Courtesy of the Ohio History Connection.*

Bottom: A close-up view of the marble Speaker's desk today, showing the moldings of the lower part of the corbel, designed by architect Nathan Kelly in 1855. The Speaker's desk and House Clerk's desk were made by Charles Rule of Cincinnati, Ohio. *Photo by Michael Rupert.*

58 THE OHIO STATEHOUSE

Left: The Speaker of the House is the highest-ranking legislator in the Ohio House of Representatives; the Speaker's office is located on the second floor of the Ohio Statehouse. *Photo by Mike Elicson.* **Bottom:** Originally providing light to the interior of the Statehouse, this former light court is now the House Members' Lounge. *Photo by Dan Shellenbarger.*

CORNERSTONE TO CUPOLA 59

THE SPEAKER'S CHAIR

Since its placement in the House Chamber, the magnificent Speaker's Chair has caused quite a bit of speculation as to who made it? And who was it made for? Beginning in the early twentieth century, visiting school children were told that it was made for Abraham Lincoln when he spoke in the House Chamber in 1861. This article from the December 10, 1878, issue of the *Columbus Dispatch* should help solve the mystery:

THE SPEAKER'S CHAIR
A Massive Piece of Furniture for the Ohio House of Representatives

"The Ohio Furniture Company, 119 and 121 South High Street, has placed in its show window the massive chair manufactured in its shops for the use of the Speaker of the Ohio House of Representatives. The back of the chair is seven feet high and is surrounded by the seal of the State, carved in black walnut. The width of the chair at the seat is two feet, six inches, and the height of the seat two feet, four inches. A foot stool ten inches high will assist the Speaker in the maintenance of ease and proper dignity. Two smaller chairs, made to match the large one, will be placed one on each side of the Speaker. Dark, red silk velvet, upholstered on soft, elastic seat springs made especially for this chair, covers the back, seat, and arms. The seal is made from a copy of the original, as found in the office of the Clerk of the Supreme Court. It has the sheaf, the arrows, the mountains, and the rising sun. All carved work on the chair was done by hand. Those who have seen the big chairs in the Capitol at Washington city say this is ahead of anything they have there in size and artistic finish. In the latter respect, it is very fine. The perspective in the carving of the seal is particularly good. Gilt is made use of in this one spot alone, to imitate the rays of the sun.

The chair was designed by Mr. A.H. Rollin, foreman of the Company's shops. Two or three men were engaged on the carving. Their time was kept, so that the price of the article will depend somewhat upon the length of time required to make it. A wreath of carved work surrounds the seal. More or less work of the same kind is associated with the design of the legs and arms. The stock of the upright pieces of the back were three-and-a-half inches in size. In the chair these pieces are worked down to three inches. Six-inch stuff was required for the legs, which, at the largest part, are carved down to five-and-a-half inches. Walnut, of course, is the kind of wood made use of. Two men were necessary to handle the chair in the trimming room. It has not been weighed. Good guessers place its weight at one hundred and fifty pounds. Notwithstanding its immense size, it is symmetrical. It was built expressly for one spot, which was measured carefully, so that the chair would be adapted to it in all respects.

The members of the House will be provided with one hundred and twenty walnut chairs, at a cost of $5.50 each. These chairs have the Gardner patent seat and back of perforated wood. The perforations in the back are in the design of a monogram of the letters O.H.R.—Ohio House of Representatives. Each chair is supplied with a spring and screw, so that the member may assume any position except a horizontal.

The corps of usual employees in the House, under the direction of Mr. Bienkner, are getting things in good order for the reception of the General Assembly, which will meet January 7, 1879."

The Speaker's Chair today, complete with the carved Great Seal of the State of Ohio and two smaller matching chairs on each side. *Photo by Mike Elicson.*

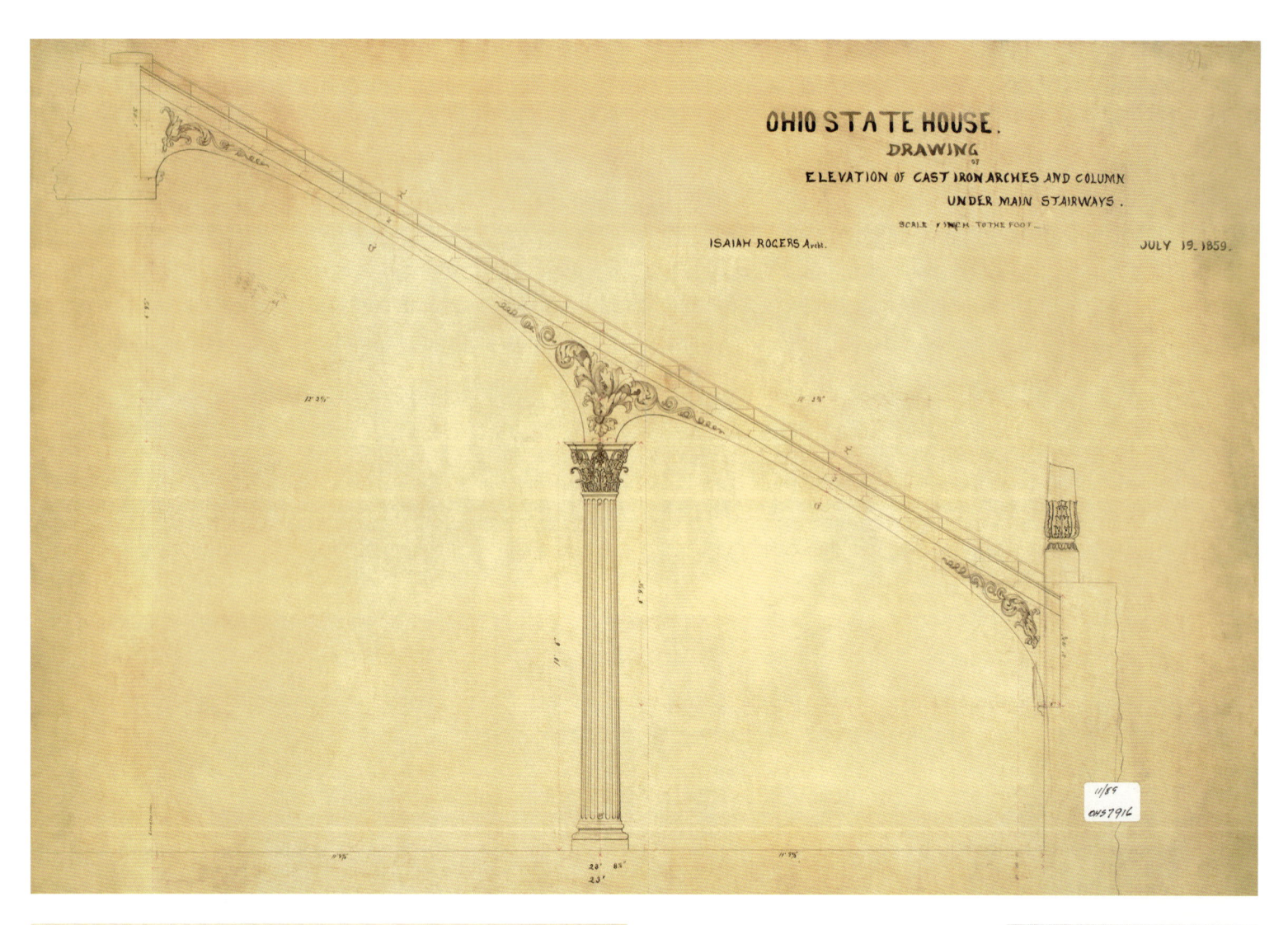

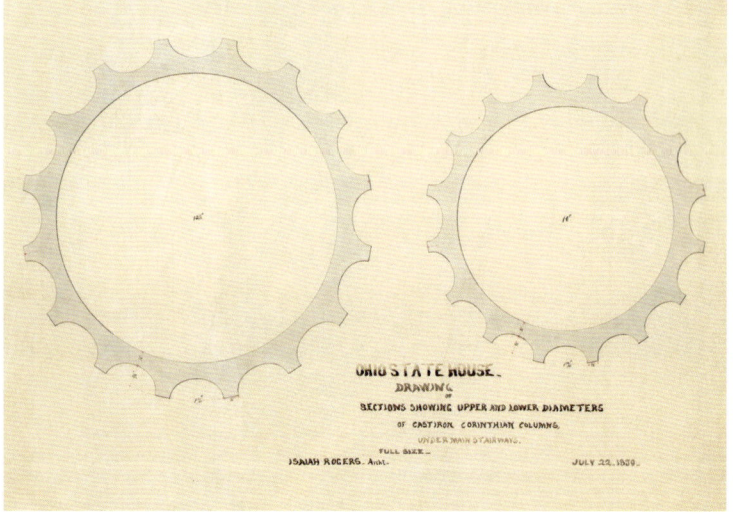

Top: Drawing of the cast iron arch that was placed under the main stairways that lead up to the Senate and House Chambers. Architect Isaiah Rogers drew this plan in July of 1859. *Courtesy of the Ohio History Connection.* **Left:** This Ohio Statehouse drawing by Architect Isaiah Rogers shows the upper and lower diameters of the cast iron Corinthian columns under the main stairways. *Courtesy of the Ohio History Connection.* **Right:** A close up view of one of the cast iron arches. *Photo by Mike Elicson.* **Facing page:** One of the cast iron arches supporting the main stairway leading up to the Senate Chamber today. A cast iron Corinthian column provides support to the arch. The handrail and balusters are made of east Tennessee and white Italian marble. *Photo by Michael Rupert.*

62 THE OHIO STATEHOUSE

CORNERSTONE TO CUPOLA 63

Below: Taken by photographer R.F. Bowdish in the 1870s, this stereograph is one of the earliest images of the Ohio Senate Chamber. *Courtesy of the Ohio History Connection.* **Bottom:** A central view of the Senate Chamber floor today. The Senate President's desk and Senate Clerk's desk are original, and were made by Charles Rule of Cincinnati, Ohio. *Photo by Michael Rupert.*

64   THE OHIO STATEHOUSE

Photo by Rob Abel.

SENATE CHAMBER

The highly decorative elements that had been originally called for in the Senate Chamber, under the direction of the architect Nathan Kelly, were omitted in favor of a more chaste appearance. In addition, the balconies or galleries for the public were removed from the plans, placing them instead on either side of the Senate Chamber floor, with an ornamental fence providing a barrier between populace and lawmakers. In appearance, the Senate Chamber more closely follows the Greek Revival style.

Top: Renovations were made on the Senate Chamber in the early 1900s. This photograph taken between 1917 and 1918, shows new desks and chairs, a raised platform, and a middle balcony which can be seen in the upper left of this image. *Capitol Square Review & Advisory Board; 2015.024.002.* **Bottom:** A modern image taken of the same view as the 1917–1918 photograph of the Senate Chamber. The raised platform and middle balcony have been removed. Seating for visitors is provided on each side of the chamber floor. *Photo by Michael Rupert. Bottom left corner photo by Mike Elicson.*

Top: The Senate president is the highest-ranking legislator in the Ohio Senate. The Senate president's office is located on the second floor of the Ohio Statehouse. *Photo by Michael Rupert.* **Bottom:** Originally providing light to the interior of the Statehouse, this former light court is now the Senate Members' Lounge. *Photo by Dan Shellenbarger.*

OHIO'S STATE FLAG (burgee)

Architect John Eisenmann (1851-1924), who designed the Cleveland Arcade in downtown Cleveland, as well as Case Western University's Main building, is also responsible for designing the Ohio State Flag. He originally designed the flag for Ohio's display at the 1901 Pan-American Exposition at Buffalo, New York. The flag's unique swallowtail design is unlike any other state flag and is properly called a burgee. Eisenmann's flag was officially adopted as the state flag by the Ohio General Assembly in 1902.

The thirteen stars grouped about the circle represent the thirteen original colonies, while the other four stars added to the peak of the triangle represent Ohio being the seventeenth state admitted to the Union. The outer white circle signifies the Northwest Territory, and the letter "O" in Ohio. The inner red circle depicts the buckeye, suggesting Ohio's famous nickname, the "Buckeye State." The large blue triangle represents Ohio's hills and valleys and the red and white stripes represent roads and waterways.

Originally designed by John Eisenmann in 1901, this Ohio State Flag in the senate president's office was first flown over the Ohio Statehouse on the opening day of the 132nd Ohio General Assembly. *Photo by Michael Rupert.*

68 THE OHIO STATEHOUSE

GOVERNOR'S OFFICE

Salmon P. Chase was the first governor of Ohio to occupy the Governor's Office at the newly constructed Ohio Statehouse. He was very pleased with the new state capitol building, stating: "In simplicity of Design, in harmony of Proportions, and in massive solidity of Structure, it stands, and may it long stand, a monument and symbol of the clear Faith, the well-ordered Institutions, and the enduring Greatness of the People whose House it is." Near the end of his term as governor, Chase ended up being a rival to Abraham Lincoln in the race to be nominated as the republican candidate for president in the 1860 election. Although he lost the bid for nomination, Chase was appointed by Lincoln to be his Secretary of the Treasury on his war time cabinet.

The governor's office today appears much as it did in 1857 when it was first complete. The desk and bookcase are the original pieces designed for the Ohio Statehouse, and first used by Salmon P. Chase. The office is noted as a Zone 1 restoration, with all modern technology carefully hidden in the furniture.

Top left: One of the earliest known images of the interior of the Statehouse; this rare stereograph by J.Q.A. Tresize of Zanesville, Ohio, shows Governor Salmon P. Chase sitting at his desk in 1857. *John and Janet Waldsmith.* **Top right:** To mourn the death of President James A. Garfield in 1881, Governor Charles Foster's office was draped in black crepe. The original gas lighting can be seen in this stereograph view. *John and Janet Waldsmith.* **Bottom:** The governor's office as it appears today with Salmon P. Chase's original desk still in use. *Photo by Michael Rupert.*

PRESIDENTIAL HEARING ROOMS

To this day, a friendly rivalry exists between the states of Ohio and Virginia. Each state claims eight United States Presidents as their own, sharing William Henry Harrison who was born in Virginia but was elected president while living in Ohio. Until the tie is broken, Ohio and Virginia are *both known* as the *Mother of Presidents*.

Beginning in the early 1840s, nearly dominating the latter half of the nineteenth century and into the early twentieth century; eight Ohioans have held the highest executive post in the country. Eight hearing rooms within the Ohio Statehouse have been re-named to honor each of these presidents. These rooms contain artifacts related to their private and professional life. The eight presidents from Ohio in order of their time in office are as follows:

★ William Henry Harrison: 1841, Ninth President of the United States from North Bend, Ohio.

★ Ulysses S. Grant: 1869–1877, Eighteenth President of the United States from Point Pleasant, Ohio.

★ Rutherford B. Hayes: 1877–1881, Nineteenth President of the United States from Delaware, Ohio.

★ James A. Garfield: 1881, Twentieth President of the United States from Orange (Moreland Hills), Ohio.

★ Benjamin Harrison: 1889–1893, Twenty-third President of the United States from North Bend, Ohio.

★ William McKinley: 1897–1901, Twenty-fifth President of the United States from Niles, Ohio.

★ William Howard Taft: 1909–1913, Twenty-seventh President of the United States from Cincinnati, Ohio.

★ Warren G. Harding: 1921–1923, Twenty-ninth President of the United States from Corsica, Ohio.

Left: Honoring the eighteenth president of the United States, the Ulysses S. Grant Presidential Hearing Room is located on the first floor of the Ohio Statehouse. Originally from Point Pleasant, Ohio, Grant served as General in Chief of the Union Army during the American Civil War. *Photo by Dan Shellenbarger.* **Below:** Speaker of the Ohio House of Representatives, Clifford A. Rosenberger, holds a press conference in the Harding Senate Briefing Room. *Photo by Mike Elicson.*

Above, facing page top, and facing page middle: Originally open to the weather, the light courts today have glass ceilings to admit sunlight into the interior of the Statehouse. *Photos by Mike Elicson.*

LIGHT COURTS

Although gas lighting had been in use since the early nineteenth century, it was distrusted for the first fifty years, and few homes and buildings were lit by this method. The Ohio Statehouse was originally designed during this period of distrust of gas lighting, consequently relying on oil lamps, candles, and natural light. Hearing rooms and offices located along the exterior walls were designed to have tall windows to let in sunlight. To solve the problem of lighting the interior rooms, the original architects had to be creative. Four open courtyards, or light courts, were created to allow sunlight to enter through the top of the building down and in through the windows of the interior rooms. These open courtyards were just that—*open* to sunlight, rain, sleet, snow, and pigeons. Limestone walkways crossed the light courts, allowing access to meeting rooms as well as rest rooms or water closets.

By the time the Ohio Statehouse construction was finished in 1861, it came complete with gas lighting. Before the nineteenth century came to a close, however, electric lighting was introduced to the city of Columbus and the state capitol. Once the Statehouse was wired for electric, the open light courts were no longer needed, and were quickly enclosed. Over time, several floors of offices were packed into the original light courts as state government grew.

Today, the north and south light courts have been cleared of office space and contain railed walkways, and elevators. The two remaining light courts contain the Ohio House and Senate Members' lounges.

Left: Limestone walkways originally crossed the open spaces of the light courts. The last remaining limestone walkway is located in the north light court—Senate side of the Ohio Statehouse. *Photo by Michael Rupert.*

CORNERSTONE TO CUPOLA 73

STATE ROOM

Located on the first floor of the Ohio Statehouse, the State Room provides a space for executive and legislative staff meetings, press conferences, and a venue for special events. Original artwork from the nineteenth century is displayed, hanging in *salon* style along the walls, and 1860s period furnishings complete the room. The State Room was originally the office of the Adjutant General of Ohio.

74 THE OHIO STATEHOUSE

The State Room provides a meeting space and a venue for press conferences and events. *Photo by Mike Elicson.*

GEORGE WASHINGTON WILLIAMS MEMORIAL ROOM

George Washington Williams was a veteran of the American Civil War, a minister, lawyer, writer, and was Ohio's first African-American state legislator. Elected to represent the citizens of Hamilton County in 1879, Williams served one term (1880–1881) in the Ohio House of Representatives, during the sixty-fourth Ohio General Assembly. Located in the southwest corner of the first floor of the Statehouse, the George Washington Williams Memorial Room honors this milestone event in Ohio history.

In 2001, artist Ed Dwight created a bust of Williams that is located in the 1880s period-furnished room. Columbus artist Ron Anderson created a painting that illustrates Representative Williams addressing the Ohio House of Representatives in 1880. Images of maps and locations that pertain to George Washington Williams' life adorn the walls alongside photographs of late nineteenth century African-American state legislators. A searchable computer kiosk is included, as well, that lists all black legislators who have served in the Ohio General Assembly.

The George Washington Williams Memorial Room is appropriately decorated with period furnishings that reflect the 1880s. *Photos by Mike Elicson.*

LADIES' GALLERY

Two years after the passage of the Nineteenth Amendment to the U.S. Constitution, which granted women the right to vote and hold public office, Ohioans elected the first six women to the state legislature. Those first women elected to the Ohio General Assembly were: Nettie Bromley Longhead, Ohio Senate, 1922–1928; Maude Comstock Waitt, Ohio Senate, 1922–1930; May Martin Van Wye, Ohio House, 1922–1928 and Ohio Senate, 1928–1930; Lulu Thomas Gleason, Ohio House, 1922–1924; Adelaide Sterling Ott, Ohio House, 1922–1928; and Nettie Mackenzie Clapp, Ohio House, 1922–1930. Framed photographs of these political ground breaking women hang in the gallery, as well as a painting of Jo Ann Davidson, the first female Speaker of the Ohio House of Representatives (1995–2000), by artist Leslie Adams.

The Ladies' Gallery is used for press conferences, meetings, and visitor education. Exhibits related to the first female legislators and the women's suffrage movement is also located in this room in the southeast corner of the first floor of the Statehouse.

The Ladies' Gallery features a portrait of Jo Ann Davidson, the first female Speaker of the Ohio House of Representatives (1995–2000), by artist Leslie Adams. *Photo by Michael Rupert.*

78 THE OHIO STATEHOUSE

Inset: Lighting in today's Crypt is provided by electric reproductions of the original gas lights. **Below:** A view of the Crypt, or Museum Gallery, from underneath one of its barrel arches. *Photos by Mike Elicson.*

MUSEUM GALLERY (CRYPT)

Located on the ground floor of the Ohio Statehouse, the Crypt exemplifies what could be termed the *bones* of the building. The white painted brick and limestone form barrel arches underneath vaulted ceilings overhead, which gives one an appreciation for the ancient classical architecture that has stood the test of time. Re-named the Museum Gallery, it was originally built to house and store fuel, workers rooms, as well as the boilers for the very first heating system at the Statehouse. Today the area is used for press conferences, historic presentations, and as a passageway for visitors and legislators entering through the underground parking garage.

The Ohio Statehouse Museum and Education Center is located in the Museum Gallery, and provides an interactive experience to students and visitors of all ages. First highlighting the Ohio Constitutions of 1802 and 1851, as well as historic political artifacts, the Museum then moves on through the three branches of government in various interactive exhibits that encourage visitor participation in Ohio's democratic process. Also located on the ground floor is the Governor Thomas Worthington Center. Established in 2013, the Worthington Center provides a classroom-like setting that is ideal for various groups and organizations who wish to hold meetings, conferences, and informational seminars. County historical societies from Ohio's eighty-eight counties are able to display artifacts and historic information related to their counties in two built-in exhibit cases, which are housed within the Worthington Center.

CORNERSTONE TO CUPOLA 79

80 THE OHIO STATEHOUSE

The Ohio Statehouse Museum and Education Center is located in the Museum Gallery, and encourages participation in Ohio's democratic process through interactive exhibits. *Photo by Mike Elicson. Top right photo by Dan Shellenbarger.*
Bottom: The Governor Thomas Worthington Center provides a venue for meetings and informational seminars. Rotating exhibits from Ohio's eighty-eight counties are housed within the center. *Photo by Mike Elicson.*

CHAIR OF HONOR

The Chair of Honor memorial was dedicated on November 19, 2016, and is located in the south light court on the ground floor. Reminding citizens to never forget the sacrifices of American military personnel who have been classified as Missing in Action or as Prisoners of War, the memorial has a plaque with the following inscription:

NEVER FORGET

The Chair of Honor is empty. It will remain so until our Missing in Action and Prisoners of War return to take their rightful place among us. From World War I to our current military conflicts there are 82,600 military personnel who stepped forward to answer our Nation's call to arms, to protect our freedoms and our way of life, for Duty, Honor, Country, never to return.

We, as a Nation, must work to bring them home to be among their families or buried on their native soil. Do Not Forget Them. They have sacrificed for us all.

Photo by Mike Elicson.

This late nineteenth century photograph shows the east side of the Ohio Statehouse before the addition of the Judiciary Annex, which was constructed from 1899–1901. Note the entrances to the Crypt on the bottom left and right sides of the Statehouse. These entrances were covered over during later remodeling efforts. *Courtesy of the Ohio History Connection.*

Photo by Mike Elicson.

84 THE SENATE BUILDING

THE Senate BUILDING

EXPANSION

Toward the end of the nineteenth century, *Ohio's state government was already feeling overcrowded within the Ohio Statehouse. In particular, this overcrowding was felt to a larger degree within the judiciary branch, which led to a request for a new space or building. Once again, numerous architects and building firms made proposals to state government once they learned that a new building was in the offing.* One particular set of architects, Yost and Packard from Columbus, proposed that an additional story be added to the top of the existing Statehouse! Another proposal that was looked on favorably by the Ohio Supreme Court was the building of wings on the north and south side of the Statehouse. The *Ohio State Journal* of January 26, 1894, carried a story about the proposed Statehouse wing: "Last evening the committee on public buildings in both branches, the Statehouse commission and several of the Supreme Court judges held a joint meeting in the senate committee room. The object was to exchange views on the proposed enlargement of the Statehouse. It can be authoritatively stated that a bill will be introduced in a few days which will provide for a special levy of 1–10 of a mill for three years on all the taxable property of the state in order to raise money to enlarge the Statehouse." Evidently the Supreme Court judges were feeling pinched in their current quarters for the same article stated that the judges advised the construction of "…the south wing at once." Despite this urging from the judges, it would be 1897 before the state legisla-

Photo by Mike Elicson.

ture would approve a design for the Judiciary Building (also known as the Judiciary Annex). Instead of wings or an additional story being added to the existing Statehouse, a separate, free-standing building was to be constructed on the eastern side of the square. This Neo-Classical style building which was designed by Samuel Hannaford & Sons, from Cincinnati, Ohio, would eventually house the Supreme Court, Clerk, Law Library, Attorney General, as well as the Agriculture, Health, Insurance, and Public Works Departments. In contrast to the Ohio Statehouse, little or no fanfare attended the laying of the cornerstone for this building on February 16, 1899. "The cornerstone of the addition to the state capitol was laid Thursday afternoon with appropriate ceremonies in the presence of a large number of people. Although the event was one in which every citizen of Ohio has an interest, there was no extraordinary demonstration." (*Ohio State Journal*, February 21, 1899.) Completed in 1901, the Ohio Supreme Court moved out of their old quarters in the Ohio Statehouse to take up official residence in their newly appointed chambers.

Four, two-story Doric columns are prominent above the entrance to the Senate Building on the east side of Capitol Square. *Photo by Dan Shellenbarger.*

THE BUILDING WITH TWO IDENTITIES

The Judiciary Building or Annex is often referred to as an addition to the Ohio Statehouse in various accounts from the time period. It would appear however that the annex was to have two identities: The east or Third Street side of the building has a *main* entrance. Visitors entering from this side of the building will note that the annex was constructed in a design that complimented the Ohio Statehouse. Columbus limestone quarried from the same quarry to build the Statehouse was used and dressed in the same fashion for the annex. Four, two-story Doric columns are prominent above the main entrance to the building, as well as a Doric entablature that is, in turn, topped with a stone balustrade. The center of the triangular shaped Doric entablature has the Great Seal of Ohio embossed upon the stone, and hidden behind the balustrade is a small square cupola which allows natural light into the building through the Grand Stair Hall. "From the exterior, this building was designed to be a 'Third Street building,' with its formal façade and entrance facing east toward the street." (*The Ohio Statehouse Master Plan*, Schooley Caldwell Associates, page 35.) Yet, it is from the interior of the building that we see the addition or annex identity of the Judiciary Building. The west side of the Judiciary Building faces the Ohio Statehouse, and has a terrace-level doorway that matches the same level of the doors leading into the east side of the capitol building. Visitors entering into the building through the west doors are presented with an impressive entrance into what was the Ohio Supreme Court. The double Grand Stair Hall with its ornate detail, marble, gilt, and elaborate paintings proclaimed Ohio's wealth and power at the turn of the century. From the tiled, mosaic-patterned floor to the white marble massive stairs, handrails, and walls leading up to the second floor; visitors were meant to be impressed. Standing at the foot of the stairways, the eye is drawn upwards past fluted stone pilasters and elaborately painted plaster walls to a coffered rectangular dome. Surrounding a stained-glass Great Seal of Ohio skylight are four painted murals by Raphael and

86 THE SENATE BUILDING

Photo by Mike Elicson

Charles Pedretti of Cincinnati, Ohio, that recall Greek mythology by presenting muse-like women as symbolic carriers of important themes. They represent the arts, manufacturing, agriculture, and justice; four themes that the designers of the Judiciary Building felt important to know about Ohio. In addition to the skylight, there are several large brass electric lamps to light the interior of the Grand Stair Hall. The second floor contained two courtrooms; one on the north and one on the south side of the building. These rooms were highly decorative, and adjoined deliberation rooms that were outfitted with gas fireplaces that came complete with marble and mahogany mantels. The State Law Library was located at the north end of the first floor, and the offices for the Clerk of Courts and the Attorney General occupied the remaining rooms on this floor as well. The Ohio Supreme Court moved out of the Judiciary Building in 1974, relocating their offices and courtrooms for a time in the Rhodes Tower across from Capitol Square, moving again to their current location at the Thomas J. Moyer Ohio Judicial Center on Front Street (formerly known as the Ohio Departments Building). Since that move, the Judiciary Building became the Senate Building. Today it is the office place of Ohio's State Senators and comes complete with north and south hearing rooms that retain their original Ohio Supreme Courtroom appearance. The old deliberation rooms that anchor the corners of the second floor have become the Majority and Minority caucus rooms of the Ohio Senate, while the State Law Library became the Senator Richard H. Finan Hearing Room—in honor of the State Senator who led the renovation of Capitol Square.

88 | THE SENATE BUILDING

Facing top: The massive marble stairways of the Grand Stair Hall in the Senate Building used to ascend to the Ohio Supreme Court Chambers. *Photo by Dan Shellenbarger.* **Facing bottom left and right:** Visitors were meant to be impressed by the double Grand Stair Hall with its ornate detail. *Photos by Mike Elicson.* **Top:** The ceiling murals of the Grand Stair Hall feature four muse-like women representing: industry, agriculture, justice, and the arts. Painted by the Pedretti Brothers of Cincinnati, they surround a stained-glass Great Seal of Ohio skylight. *Photo by Mike Elicson.* **Bottom:** A close up view of the stained-glass Great Seal of Ohio skylight in the Grand Stair Hall. *Photo by Dan Shellenbarger. Cut out photo by Mike Elicson.*

Right: An early 1900s photograph of the south Supreme Courtroom showing the Justices sitting at the bench. A bailiff can be seen standing to the right of the bench. *Courtesy of the Ohio History Connection.* **Bottom:** Retaining its original Supreme Courtroom appearance, the south Senate Hearing Room today is a location for Senate committee meetings and public testimonials. *Photo by Mike Elicson.*

Top photo by Mike Elicson. **Bottom:** Decorative gold leaf highlights can be seen on the walls of the north Senate Hearing Room. *Photo by Dan Shellenbarger.*

92 THE SENATE BUILDING

Top left and right: The old Supreme Court deliberation rooms have become the Senate Majority and Minority Caucus Rooms. *Photos by Dan Shellenbarger.* **Bottom:** The former State Law Library is now the Richard H. Finan Hearing Room, named in honor of the former Senate president who led the renovation of Capitol Square. *Photo by Mike Elicson.*

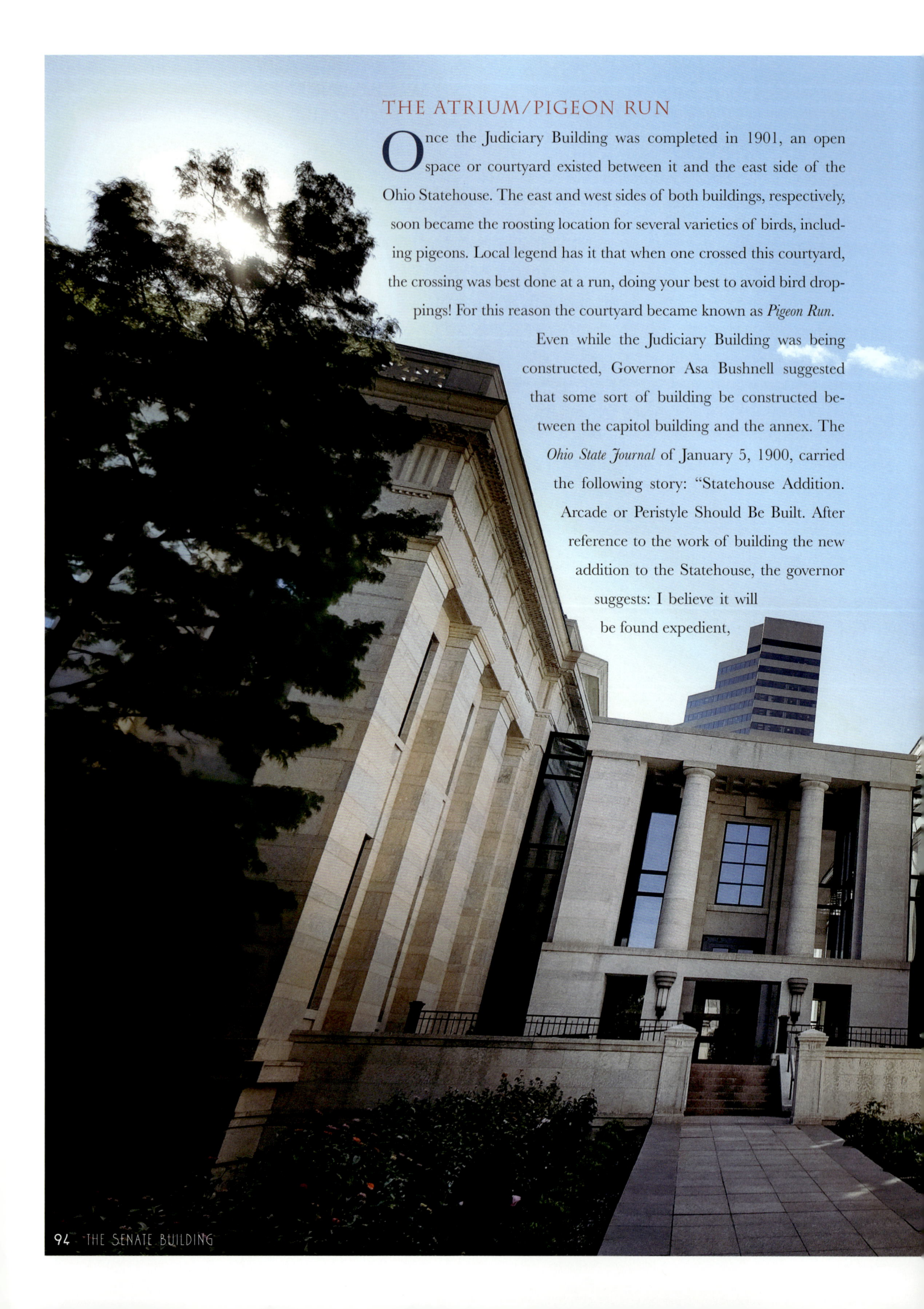

THE ATRIUM/PIGEON RUN

Once the Judiciary Building was completed in 1901, an open space or courtyard existed between it and the east side of the Ohio Statehouse. The east and west sides of both buildings, respectively, soon became the roosting location for several varieties of birds, including pigeons. Local legend has it that when one crossed this courtyard, the crossing was best done at a run, doing your best to avoid bird droppings! For this reason the courtyard became known as *Pigeon Run*.

Even while the Judiciary Building was being constructed, Governor Asa Bushnell suggested that some sort of building be constructed between the capitol building and the annex. The *Ohio State Journal* of January 5, 1900, carried the following story: "Statehouse Addition. Arcade or Peristyle Should Be Built. After reference to the work of building the new addition to the Statehouse, the governor suggests: I believe it will be found expedient,

Pigeon Run was the name given to the open space between the Ohio Statehouse (right), and the Senate Building (left), now occupied by the Atrium (center). *Photo by Mike Elicson.*

to make some provision for a connection in the form of an arcade or peristyle, which will not only add to the beauty of the whole, but be of great convenience for all." Governor Bushnell's suggestion took hold a little under one hundred years later in 1993, when the Atrium was completed. Created in a style that is neither Greek Revival nor Neo-classical, the Atrium is more of a compromise that exhibits similar materials (stone) and scale (size) that are harmonious with the Ohio Statehouse and Senate Building. Today the Atrium is the location of numerous special events at Capitol Square. Nonprofit groups often meet here to celebrate, confirm, proclaim, or discuss their own goals and identities. This kind of activity makes explicit the idea that citizens can join together to influence government, and can approach the seat of government to exercise their rights as citizens.

The Atrium is a harmonious blend of architecture that compliments both the Ohio Statehouse and the Senate Building. *Photos by Mike Elicson.*

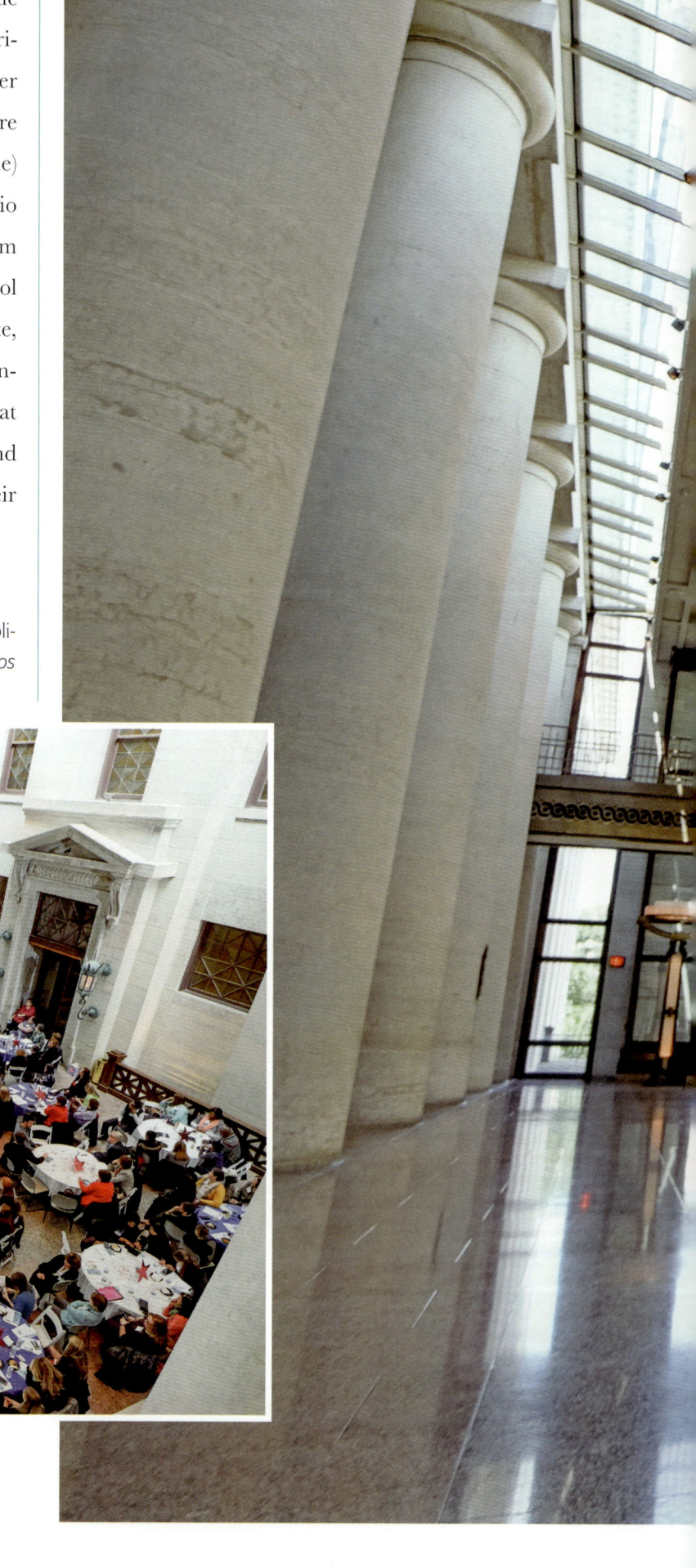

96 THE SENATE BUILDING

CORNERSTONE TO CUPOLA 97

THE MAP ROOM

Completed in 1993, the Map Room is the unofficial crossroads of Capitol Square. It is a busy passageway located on the ground floor directly between the 1861 Ohio Statehouse and the 1901 Judiciary Building (now the Senate Building). It is also a gathering place for visitors and a venue for organizations to display creative and informative exhibits. The room gets its name from the colorful twenty by twenty foot marble map of Ohio on the center floor. The map is scaled at approximately eleven inches to ten miles, meaning a person five feet, six inches tall would stand about sixty miles tall in relation to the map. As marble is not native to the state of Ohio, six different varieties of marble from around the world were used to make the map: Clear Carthage, Vermont Verde Antique, Breccla Onlclata, Tennessee Pink, Dark Cedar, and Light Emperador.

Located on the south side walls of the Map Room are two bronze bas-relief sculptures created by sculptor George Danhires of Kent, Ohio. The sculptures are gifts from the State Teacher's Retirement System and represent the *Historic Classroom* and the *Modern Classroom*. In describing his sculptures Mr. Danhires stated that "both reliefs portray experiences provided to students by dedicated and caring educators as well as to give reference to cultural influences, important historical figures, and Ohio educational innovations." Contrasting education of the past by showing old tools and methods, with present techniques including the teacher who signs "to learn," both reliefs feature Ohio objects and people including McGuffey Readers and inventors Orville and Wilbur Wright.

Also located in the Map Room is the Statehouse Museum Shop. Featuring products made by Ohio artists and vendors, the Museum Shop carries a wide selection of items including political gifts from both sides of the aisle. Shoppers can purchase a State of Ohio flag that has been officially flown over the Statehouse as well as browse through food and wine selections from the Buckeye state.

Top: The State Teacher's Retirement System commissioned the sculptures *Historic Classroom* and *Modern Classroom* by George Danhires. *Photos by Dan Shellenbarger.*

Right: This twenty by twenty foot marble map of Ohio was a gift from all eighty-eight Ohio county commissioners to the State of Ohio, in 1993. *Photo by Michael Rupert.*

MARION
LICKING
MORGAN
FRANKLIN
FAIRFIELD
HOCKING
MEIGS
MADISON
ROSS
JACKSON
CLARK
FAYETTE
LAWRENCE
GREENE
CLINTON
HIGHLAND
ADAMS
WARREN
BROWN
CLERMONT
HAMILTON

100 GROUNDS & MONUMENTS

GROUNDS & Monuments

The legendary west lawn of the Ohio Statehouse has been consistently used throughout the years as a location for citizens to hold demonstrations, political rallies, celebrations, and commemorations. In particular, commemorative events have taken place throughout the grounds of the capitol from its earliest history. Tangible evidence of these events is in the form of numerous monuments on the Statehouse yard to Ohio's political and military leaders, as well as soldiers, both men and women, who have served in the armed forces. These visible reminders of courage, hardship, and sacrifice provide inspiration for present and future generations.

THESE ARE MY JEWELS

Originally unveiled at the World's Columbian Exposition in Chicago, Illinois, on September 14, 1893, *These Are My Jewels* is located on the northwest corner of Capitol Square. The monument was created by sculptor Levi T. Scofield, a former Union Army officer who had previously created the Sailors and Soldiers Monument in Cleveland, Ohio. After its initial unveiling at the Chicago World's Fair grounds, it was moved to its present location. Ohio soldiers and statesmen,

Left: *These Are My Jewels* is located on the northwest corner of Capitol Square. *Photo by Mike Elicson.* **Bottom right:** A close-up view of Union General Philip Henry Sheridan on the *These Are My Jewels* monument sculpted by Levi T. Scofield, a former Union Army officer. *Photo by Mike Elicson.*

CORNERSTONE TO CUPOLA   101

surround a shaft topped by a statue of Cornelia, the Roman matron. Her words, "These Are My Jewels," stand out in relief at the top of the shaft. The soldiers and statesmen are: Ulysses S. Grant, William T. Sherman, Philip H. Sheridan, Edwin M. Stanton, James A. Garfield, and Salmon P. Chase. When the monument was moved to the Ohio Statehouse grounds in 1894, former Ohio General, Governor, and President of the United States Rutherford B. Hayes was added at the request of then-Ohio Governor William McKinley. The line, "These Are My Jewels," is taken from an anecdote from Roman history about Cornelia, a highly respected woman who considered her sons to be her jewels, or greatest possession. This is the tallest monument on Capitol Square with an overall height of thirty-one feet.

This photograph shows the *These Are My Jewels* monument at the Chicago World's Fair Grounds in 1893, before it was moved to the grounds of the Ohio Statehouse. *Courtesy of the Ohio History Connection. Cut out photo by Mike Elicson.*

WILLIAM MCKINLEY MONUMENT

William McKinley, former Ohio Governor and twenty-fifth President of the United States, was shot twice in the abdomen by an anarchist, Leon Czolgosz, on September 6, 1901, at the Pan-American Exposition in Buffalo, New York. McKinley died eight days later due to gangrene caused by the gunshot wounds. In 1906, the McKinley monument was erected to honor the martyred president. A New York sculptor, H.A. MacNeil created the monument which is located on the west side of Capitol Square along High Street. The monument features an elevated, life-size figure of William McKinley flanked by two groups of people: a mother with her daughter representing Peace—symbolic of McKinley's quick resolution of the Spanish-American War; and a father with his son representing Prosperity due to the economic recovery from the Panic of 1893. According to the *Ohio State Journal* of March 14, 1905, "McKinley's features will be as they were when he delivered the Buffalo speech." President McKinley had made an address on September 5, the day before he was assassinated. The monument has McKinley represented with a manuscript in hand as if delivering his speech to the crowds at Buffalo, New York.

New York sculptor H. A. MacNeil created the William McKinley Monument, located on the west lawn of Capitol Square. *Photo by Mike Elicson.*

Manuscript in hand, McKinley was sculpted to look as if he was delivering a speech. *Photo by Mike Elicson.*

Inscription:

William McKinley

Twenty-Fifth President of the United States

Let us ever remember that our interest is in concord, not conflict, and that our real eminence rests in the victories of peace, not those of war.

Our earnest prayer is that God will graciously vouchsafe prosperity, happiness and peace to all our neighbors, and like blessings to all the peoples and powers of earth.

The fame of such a man will shine like a beacon through the mists of ages—an object of reverence, of imitation, and of love.

PEACE

Commissioned by the Woman's Relief Corps of Ohio, the statue *Peace* honors Ohio men's and women's sacrifices and contributions during the American Civil War. The monument features a winged angelic-like female, juxtaposed with the weapons of war and an olive branch of peace. Created by sculptor Bruce Wilder Saville, and dedicated in 1923, the statue is located on the north side of Capitol Square along Broad Street.

Photos by Mike Elicson.

Inscription:

Commemorating the heroic sacrifices of Ohio's soldiers of the Civil War 1861–65 and the loyal women of that period.

Erected by the Woman's Relief
Corps Department of Ohio
1923

PEACE

COMMEMORATING THE HEROIC SACRIFICES OF OHIO'S SOLDIERS OF
THE CIVIL WAR 1861-65 AND THE LOYAL WOMEN OF THAT PERIOD

ERECTED BY THE WOMAN'S RELIEF CORPS DEPARTMENT OF OHIO
1923

When our country sent out the call to arms for the preservation of the Union, Ohio sent more than three hundred thousand of her sons…They had faith that right makes might and that faith dared to do their duty…This memorial is erected in grateful tribute to their devotion and self-sacrifice.

Men win glory in the fierce heat of conflict but the glory of Woman is more hardly won…Upon her falls the burden of maintaining the family and the home; nursing the sick and wounded and restoring the courage of the broken. She endures the suspense of battle without its exaltation…This memorial is erected in grateful tribute to the loyal women of 61–65 without whose help no victory—or lasting peace—could ever have been won.

Let us have peace.

CORNERSTONE TO CUPOLA   105

THE OHIO SQUIRREL HOUSE

The beautiful and organized *park-like* grounds of the Ohio Statehouse hearken back to its original wilderness appearance. The grounds earliest descriptions describe it as being well-timbered with a variety of trees such as beech, hickory, maple, and oak. In 1815, shortly before the first Statehouse and public buildings at Columbus were constructed, Governor Thomas Worthington contracted with a local man to remove the native timber from the square. After that, the square at various times was farmed, raising corn and wheat, as well as used as a pasture for local farmers who drove their cows down to the capitol for a snack. Pasturing on the Ohio Statehouse grounds was a problem for years to come as evidenced by this article contained in the June 15, 1881, issue of the *Ohio State Journal*: "A drove of cows came over from the West Side last night and held a lawn fete in the State House yard. It was strawberries and cream to them, and they continued their banquet till daylight." Although cows are no longer pastured on the Statehouse grounds, squirrels, which made their presence known in the late 1800s, are still seen today in the Statehouse yard. As the Statehouse neared its completion in 1861, particular attention was paid to landscaping and improving the grounds. The grounds were leveled. Grass seed was planted as well as a variety of trees and shrubs, essentially making the grounds a large public park. This provided an excellent habitat for the Eastern gray squirrel (Sciurus carolinensis), which among other items enjoys a diet of tree bark, acorns, and walnuts. On May 15, 1894, the *Ohio State Journal* mentioned that, "Some time last week a strange squirrel was turned loose in the Capitol grounds. Last Saturday and yesterday it bit several persons and the employees of the yard were compelled to kill it." Despite the removal of this one squirrel from the grounds, it is evident that their populations continued to not only flourish but were well-fed, as well. Superintendent of State House and Grounds, H.A. Axline stated in his annual report to the governor in 1897 that "The squirrels, to the number of more than half a hundred are fat and sleek." Indeed it would seem that squirrels were to be encouraged to stay on the grounds and even have their own house to reside within. "Squirrels To Have A House. The statehouse yard is to have a new squirrel house. William H. Horden of Middleport has constructed a miniature residence, modeled upon modern ideas, which will be given to the state for the use of the squirrels. Though only about four feet square the structure has every feature of a modern residence. It has five rooms, with front and rear porches, gables and chimneys. The windows can be moved up and down and the doors open and close. The structure is made of wood but represents an excellent imitation of pressed brick in the first story." (*Ohio State Journal*, June 5, 1903.)

Now in their third century at the Ohio Statehouse, the squirrels, it appears, are here to stay.

A squirrel perches on a man's knee in this 1902 photograph on the west lawn of the Ohio Statehouse grounds. *Capitol Square Review & Advisory Board; 2011.001.001.*

Facing page: Speaker of the Ohio House of Representatives, Clifford A. Rosenberger (center), breaks ground for a tree planting during the Earth Day celebration at the Ohio Statehouse in 2016. *Photo by Mike Elicson.*

CORNERSTONE TO CUPOLA 107

SPIRIT OF '98

Located on the west front lawn of the Ohio Statehouse, the *Spirit of '98* commemorates the soldiers who fought in the Spanish-American War, Philippine Insurrection, and the China Relief Expedition (1898–1902). Sculpted by Frank L. Jirouch, it was commissioned by the State of Ohio and the United Spanish War Veterans Memorial Commission.

Inscription:

Erected by the State of Ohio to the honor and memory of the Ohio veterans of the Spanish-American War, Philippine Insurrection and the China Relief Expedition.

1898–1902

The cause which triumphed through their valor will live.

United Spanish War Veterans, 1898–1902 * Cuba, Philippine Islands, Puerto Rico, U.S.A.

The Republic is secure so long as we continue to honor the memory of its defenders.

United Spanish War Veterans Memorial Commission appointed by Governor Vic Donahey. Authorized by the 87th General Assembly of Ohio.

Carmi A. Thompson * Charles F. Thompson * Ralph H. Carroll * Frank Auth * Thomas W. Jones * Frank D. Henderson * George F. Schlesinger * Ernest P. Hazard * George M. Forney

"We make immortal the principles for which they contended." —Edward S. Matthian, Commander, Department of Ohio, United Spanish War Veterans.

1928 by United Spanish War Veterans Memorial Commission (Ohio).

The *Spirit of '98* commemorates the soldiers who fought in the Spanish-American War, Philippine Insurrection, and the China Relief Expedition (1898–1902). *Photo by Mike Elicson.*

The *Spirit of '98* has been standing guard on the west lawn of the Ohio Statehouse since its dedication in 1928. *Photos by Mike Elicson.*

The *Ohio World War Memorial* is located on the west lawn near the entrance to the Ohio Statehouse. Photos by Mike Elicson.

OHIO WORLD WAR MEMORIAL

Designed and created by Arthur Ivone in 1930, the *Ohio World War Memorial* is dedicated to the American soldiers who served in World War I. Often referred to as the *Doughboy*, which is a period reference to American soldiers during this conflict; the monument is located near the front entrance to the Statehouse on the west front lawn.

Inscription:

Ohio World War Memorial
1917–1918

To justice in war and lasting peace after victory.

To the Armed Forces of the United States "with the going down of the sun and in the morning we shall remember them."

To the women of America in the World War. They served nobly in a just cause.

Authorized by an Act of the 88th General Assembly of Ohio. Myers Y. Cooper, Governor.

Dedicated November 22, 1930—Commission: Chas. W. Montgomery, Miss Pauline F. Abrams, Arthur W. Reynolds, Horace S. Keifer, Gilson D. Light, R.G. Ingersoll.

The Italian navigator Christopher Columbus made four voyages of discovery to the new world. The *Christopher Columbus Discovery Monument* is located on the southwest corner of Capitol Square. *Photo by Mike Elicson.*

CHRISTOPHER COLUMBUS DISCOVERY MONUMENT

Originally commissioned for the Pontifical College Josephinum in Columbus, Ohio, by Monsignor Joseph Jessing in 1892, the statue was moved to the Statehouse yard in 1932. Designed by sculptor Alphons Pelzer, the explorer Christopher Columbus is featured holding a globe in his left hand, and represented as a man of thought and mind, rather than a man of action. The monument is located on the southwest corner of Capitol Square.

Inscription:
Base West side: Christopher Columbus, an Italian navigator, launched four voyages of discovery to the new world.

East side: Donated by the Josephinum to the State of Ohio. This statue was relocated to Capitol Square.

North side: The fountain honors Ohio's sister state bond with Liguria, Italy, the navigator's home.

South side: The Pontifical College Josephinum commissioned the statue from the W.H. Mullins studio.

Fountain West side: 1492. The spirit of discovery has the power to change the course of human history as demonstrated by the voyages of Christopher Columbus, whose imagination shattered the boundaries of the Western world. Modern history has been shaped by one man's courage to pursue a dream. 1892. A dream shared by later generations who explored a vast continent where freedom and opportunity beckoned to those with the courage and imagination to venture westward. 1932. Westward into Ohio came the successors to the spirit of Columbus, naming the capitol city of the new state after the man who symbolized the spirit of the frontier…1992. Frontiers explored by later generations of Ohioans extend beyond land and water to a new world whose potential remains to be unlocked by the spirit of discovery.

OHIO VETERANS PLAZA

Designed by Schooley Caldwell Associates of Columbus, Ohio, the *Ohio Veterans Plaza* was officially dedicated on August 22, 1998. It was built to honor Ohio's men and women who have served our country since World War II, as well as those who will serve in the future. On the day of the dedication, State Senator Eugene Watts delivered a speech in which he stated: "Indeed, it is hard to recall this day, that until this day, there was no state monument to the veterans of World War II, Korea, Vietnam, and also the recent Persian Gulf War." It had been more than sixty years since the last veterans memorial had been planned or created at Capitol Square. The project to create this memorial was overseen by the Department of Veterans Affairs and the Capitol Square Review and Advisory Board, as well as an advisory committee of Ohio veterans.

Anonymous excerpts from letters written to loved ones left behind by soldiers from all five branches of the military are the main focus of the monument. There are seventy letters, etched in two curved, ten feet high Ohio limestone walls. "The letters helped those left behind get through the war," said a former Ohio Marine Corps veteran of the South Pacific who was quoted in *The Plain Dealer* of Saturday, August 22, 1998. The monument,

Below: Built to honor Ohio's men and women who have served our country since World War II, as well as those who will serve in the future, the *Ohio Veterans Plaza* was officially dedicated on August 22, 1998. *Photo by Dan Shellenbarger.* **Facing page:** Members of the U.S. Armed Forces place a wreath at the annual Governor's Wreath Laying Ceremony on Memorial Day at the *Ohio Veterans Plaza. Photos by Mike Elicson.*

which was designed to be a main entrance into the east side of the Capitol, also features two fountains flanked by benches and flowers. Designations of the five branches of the armed services inscribed with names of Ohio's eighty-eight counties with accompanying flagpoles, as well as flagpoles displaying the United States, Ohio, and POW/MIA flags, are all arranged on a large grassy lawn to commemorate the traditional parade ground atmosphere of a military post. The *Ohio Veterans Plaza* is located on the east side of Capitol Square along Third Street.

OHIO HOLOCAUST AND LIBERATORS MEMORIAL

The *Ohio Holocaust and Liberators Memorial* was unveiled by Governor John Kasich and architect Daniel Libeskind during a ceremony held on June 2, 2014. The ceremony was the conclusion of a three-year process that began May 4, 2011, when Governor Kasich proposed a memorial to remember Ohio Holocaust survivors and Ohio World War II veterans who liberated Nazi death camps. In March 2012, Governor Kasich signed legislation authorizing the creation of a memorial with oversight of the project being given to the Capitol Square Review and Advisory Board and the Ohio Arts Council. The mission of the Memorial states: "…to create a memorial that would help public officials and visitors to the Statehouse understand not just the history of the Holocaust, but the fact that today we must continue to stand against evil. This Memorial will remind people about man's inhumanity to man. It is a monument to remember the victims of the Holocaust, Ohio survivors, and liberators. The Memorial should inspire people to think and act differently in the face of hatred, anti-Semitism and genocide as well as motivate visitors to learn more about the topic and to serve as a springboard for other educational activities." The memorial is located on the south side of Capitol Square.

Inscribed limestone wall (inside face):
INSPIRED BY THE OHIO SOLDIERS WHO WERE PART OF THE AMERICAN LIBERATION AND SURVIVORS WHO MADE OHIO THEIR HOME

IF YOU SAVE ONE LIFE, IT IS AS IF YOU SAVED THE WORLD —The Talmud

IN REMEMBRANCE OF THE SIX MILLION JEWS WHO PERISHED IN THE HOLOCAUST AND MILLIONS MORE INCLUDING PRISONERS OF WAR, ETHNIC AND RELIGIOUS MINORITIES, FREEMASONS, HOMOSEXUALS, THE MENTALLY ILL, DEVELOPMENTALLY DISABLED, AND POLITICAL DISSIDENTS WHO SUFFERED UNDER NAZI GERMANY

The *Ohio Holocaust and Liberators Memorial* is located on the south side of Capitol Square. *Photo by Mike Elicson.*

Inscribed limestone wall (top surface):

"Every human being who chooses to remember this chapter of history and to infuse it with meaning is thereby choosing to struggle for the preservation of the bedrock moral values that alone make possible the existence of a well-ordered society. This is a commitment to uphold human rights, above all, freedom and the sanctity of life, and the opportunity for people to live side by side in harmony."

—Avner Shalev

Photo by Mike Elicson.

CORNERSTONE TO CUPOLA 117

Monument Inscription:

STARS

Michael Schwartz arrived in Auschwitz-Birkenau in August of 1944 with one of the last transports from the Lodz ghetto. Though a veteran of this first and last ghetto of Nazi Europe, Michael was in a state of shock when he was shoved out of the cattle car into the Auschwitz kingdom. The railway platform with its barking dogs, screaming S.S. men, kicking guards, and the sorrowful eyes of quick-moving prisoners in striped uniforms inspired terror, hopelessness, and a strange wish to get it over and done with as quickly as possible. Before he realized what was happening, he was separated from his family and was led away in the opposite direction with a group of young men. The men marched beneath a barrage of leather truncheons, near the edges of flaming pits where people were tossed alive. The air was filled with sulfur and the stench of burning flesh.

A few hours later, his hair shaven, his body stinging from disinfectants, wearing a striped, oversized uniform and a pair of skimpy broken clogs, Michael, along with hundreds of young men, was led off to the barracks. There in the barracks, he found a cousin from whom he had been separated earlier at the platform. Only after looking at his cousin did Michael realize the transformation that he himself had undergone since his arrival on that accursed platform. That night in the barracks the cousins promised each other never to part again. It was the first decision Michael had made since his arrival at Auschwitz.

Michael quickly learned the realities of Auschwitz. Survival depended on one's ability to "organize" anything and everything, from an additional sip of coffee to a better sleeping place on the three-tiered wooden planks; and of course one had to present a healthy and useful appearance if one hoped to pass selections.

One day, rumors spread in Michael's barracks that the impending selection was of particular importance, for those selected would be transferred out of Auschwitz to work at another camp. Michael was especially anxious to pass that selection. In the few months he had been in Auschwitz he had learned that Auschwitz would eventually devour everybody, even those who deciphered its survival code.

The moment came. Michael and his cousin stood in front of Mengele, whose clean, shaven face glittered in the sun and whose eyes shone. The angel of death was in his moment of bliss. Michael's turn came and Mengele's finger pointed: "Right!" Then Michael heard Mengele's death sentence on his cousin: "Left!"

A moment later Michael stood before a table where three people sat dressed in white coats. One was holding

118 GROUNDS & MONUMENTS

Ohio Governor John Kasich at the unveiling of the Ohio Holocaust and Liberators Memorial on June 2, 2014. *Photo by Mike Elicson.*

a stamp pad, one a huge rubber stamp, and the third a pen and a white sheet of paper. Michael felt the cold rubber stamp press against his forehead and saw a pen mark a line on the white sheet of paper.

Michael moved onto a group of young men, all naked like himself, wearing only a huge ink star on their foreheads. Michael realized that this star was the passport that would take him out of the camp, and that his cousin in the other group just a few meters away would be taken to the chimneys.

In the commotion of the selection Michael decided to act. He walked briskly over to his cousin, spat on his cousin's forehead, pressed his own forehead against his cousin's, took his cousin by the hand, and led him to the group marked with stars. Only then did he dare look at his cousin. There in the middle of his forehead was the imprint of the lucky star, the passport that would lead them out of the Auschwitz hell.

From Birkenau, Michael and his cousin were transported to Neuengamme, Braunschweig, Watenstadt, Beendorf, Ravensbruck, and Ludwigslust, where they slaved in the Hermann Goering works (factories) in private German companies engaged in the war industry.

On a May day in 1945, a tank entered a camp near Ludwigslust. On it was painted a huge white star and inside the tank sat a black-faced soldier wearing a steel helmet. After six years in the Nazi slave kingdom, Michael and his cousin were once again free men.

CORNERSTONE TO CUPOLA   119

Photo by Mike Elicson.

Index

A

Abrams, Bazil, 3
Abrams House, 3, *4*
Abrams, Pauline F., 110
Adams, Leslie, 77
Adams, W.A., 11
Adena Mansion and Gardens Society, 5
American Civil War, ix, 24, 26, 33, 38, 71, 76, 104
American Revolution, 13
Anderson, Ron, 76
The Architect's Dream (Cole), 12
The Atrium, 32, 94, *95–96*
Auschwitz-Birkenau, 118–119
Auth, Frank, 108
Axline, H.A., 106

B

Badger, Ephraim, 17
Barclay, Robert, 38
Black Hawk Braves, 13
Bowdish, R.F., 64
Burry, Richard W., 35
Bushnell, Asa, 94, 96

C

Capitol Café, 33
Capitol Festival, 21
Capitol Square, 5, *9*, 10, *14*, 21, *27*, *30*, 31, 33, 42, 66, *86*, 87, 93, 96, 98, *101–103*, 104, 106, *111*, 112, *113*, 114
Capitol Square Renovation Foundation, 32
Capitol Square Review & Advisory Board, 33, 112, 114
Carroll, Ralph H., 108
Central Ohio Lunatic Asylum, 10
Chair of Honor, 82, *83*
Chase, Salmon P., *21*, *102*
Chicago World's Fair, 101, *102*
Chillicothe courthouse, 3, *4*, 5–7, 18
China Relief Expedition, 108
Christopher Columbus Discovery Monument (Pelzer), *111*, 112
Christy, Howard Chandler, 37, 39
Clapp, Nettie Mackenzie, 77
Cole, Thomas, 10–13
Columbus Dispatch
    English John Robinson and, 29
    Speaker's Chair and, 60–61
    William "Billy" Addison Ireland and, *42*
Columbus Statehouse, *6*, 7
Constitution, ix, 4, 15, 77, 79
Cooper, Myers Y., 110
Cornelia, *102*
Creighton, William, 5
The Crypt, *16*, 17–18, 49, *78–79*, 82
Cummings, A. L., 10, 13, 15, 18
Cupola, ix, 3, 18–20, *22*, 24, 33, *44–47*, *49*, 86
Czolgosz, Leon, 103

D

Danhires, George, 98
Davidson, Jo Ann, 77
Davis, Alexander Jackson, 12–13
Dawn of a New Light (Christy), *39*
Declaration of Independence, 13, 15
Dennison, William, 25, *26*
Department of Veterans Affairs, 112
Deshler, Wm. G., 21
Donahey, Vic, 108
Doughboy (Ivone), *110*
Douglas, Stephen, 25

E

Edison, Thomas Alva, 38, 40
Elicson, Mike, vi, viii, 3, 5, 9, 14, 19–20, 26, 34–36, 40–41, 43, 46–50, 53–56, 59, 61–62, 66, 71–72, 75–76, 79, 81, 83, 87, 89–91, 93, 95–96, 102–104, 106, 108–112, 114, 116, 119, 120
Excelsior Shoe Company Fine Shoes, *32*

F

Fallen Timbers, battle of, 37
Finan, Richard H., 31
Foos, Joseph, 6
Forney, George M., 108
Foster, Charles, 51, 69
Frank Leslie's Illustrated Newspaper, 26
Freemasons, 13, 114

G

Garfield, James A., 69–70, *102*
Garth's Auctioneers & Appraisers, 26
General Assembly, 4, 7, 32, *50*, 61, *68*, 76–77, 108, 110
Gleason, Lulu Thomas, 77
Glenn, Jr., John H., ix, 33, *36*

Gordon, George H., 29
governor's office, 6, *69*
Gov.'s Wreath Laying Ceremony, *112*
Grand Stair Hall, 86–87, *89*
Grant, Ulysses S., *40*, 70–71, *102*
Great Black Swamp, 37
Great Seal of Ohio, *5, 35*, 86, *89*
Greek Revival architecture, 10, 18, 32–33, 44, 65, 96
Guthrie, William, 3
Gwinn, N., 7

H

Hampson, James, 4
Harding Senate Briefing Room, *71*
Harding, Warren G., 70
Harmar, Josiah, 37
Harris, Francis, 24
Harrison, Benjamin, 70
Harrison, William Henry, 70
Hayes, Rutherford B., 52, 70, 102
Hazard, Ernest P., 108
Henderson, Frank D., 108
Hermann Goering works, 119
Historical and Philosophical Society of Ohio, 15
Historic Classroom (Danhires), 98
History of Franklin County (Martin), 7
Horden, William H., 106
House Chamber floor plan, *51*
House Chamber, ix, 19, 26, 31–32, *51–54, 56, 60, 62*
House Members' Lounge, *59*
House Speaker's office, *59*
Hudson River School, 12

I

Ingersoll, R.G., 110
Ireland, William "Billy" Addison, 42
Ivone, Arthur, 110

J

Jessing, Joseph, 111
J.H. Riley & Co., 21
Jirouch, Frank L., 108
Johnston, James, 4
Jones, T.D., 41
Jones, Thomas Dow, 40
Jones, Thomas W., 108
Judiciary Building, 86–87, 94, 98

K

Kasich, John, 114, *119*
Keifer, Horace S., 110
Kelly, Nathan B., 17–20, 51, 56, 58, 65
Kerr, John, 4
Korean War, 112

L

Ladies' Gallery, *77*
Lake Erie, battle of, 38
Lancaster Guards, 13
Legislative Services Commission Bill Room, 32
Libbey, Florence Scott, 12
Libeskind, Daniel, 114
Light, Gilson D., 110
Lincoln, Abraham, ix, 21, 25–26, *27*, 40, *41*, 42, 60, 69
Lincoln and Soldiers' Monument, 40, *41*
Lincoln-Douglas debates, 25
Little Turtle, 37
Longhead, Nettie Bromley, 77
Loversidge, Robert D., 28
Ludlow, William, *6*

M

MacNeil, H.A., 103
Map Room, *98–99*

Marine Corps, *36*, 112
Martin, William T., 7
Matthian, Edward S., 108
McGuffey Readers, 98
McKinley, William, 36, 70, 102–104
McLaughlin, Alexander, 4
Mishikinikwa, 37
Modern Classroom (Danhires), 98
Montgomery, Chas. W., 110
Morrow, Jeremiah, 13, 15
Mt. Logan, 5
Museum and Education Center, *79–81*
Museum Gallery, *78–81*
Museum Shop, 98
Mutchler, Dwight, 39

N

New York State Library, 10
New York Times, fire at the old Ohio Statehouse and, 18
Nineteenth Amendment, 77

O

Ohio Arts Council, 114
Ohio Constitution, 4, 79
Ohio Departments Building, 87
Ohio Eagle, 3, *4*
Ohio Government Telecommunications, 33
Ohio History Connection, 4, 6–7, 9, 16, 21–22, 25, 27, 36, 51–52, 58, 62, 64, 82, 90, 102
Ohio Holocaust and Liberators Memorial (Libeskind), *114–119*
Ohio Monument Association, 40
Ohio Penitentiary, 10
Ohio's Capitols at Columbus, 10
Ohio State Flag, *68*
Ohio Statehouse

access door to the cistern and, *20*
architects and, 16–20
architectural drawing of the crypt and, *16*
Carte de visite of Abraham Lincoln's catafalque and, *27*
cast iron Corinthian columns and, *62–63*
cornerstone and, *14*, 15
cost of, 24
The Crypt and, *16*, 17–18, 49, *78–79*, *82*
Cupola and, ix, 3, 18–20, *22*, 24, 33, *44–47*, 49, 86
decline and renovation of, 30–32
delays and, 15–16
design competition and, 13
dimensions of, 24, *25*
Doric columns and, *86*
earliest known images of the interior and, *69*
electric lighting and, *54*
fire at the old statehouse and, 18
florid detailing of the interior and, *56–58*
glass and steel oculus of, *47*
light courts and, *72–73*
limestone staircase and, *46*, 49, *50*
limestone walkways, 72, *73*
Map Room and, *98–99*
Museum Gallery and, *78–81*
observation deck and, *48*, 49
oldest known photograph and, *22*
public balcony galleries and, *54–55*
removal of the hand-carved black walnut finishings and, 29
Rotunda and, ix, 5, 18–21, 23–24, 26, *27*, 32, *33–36*, 37, 40, *42*
Senate president's office and, *67–68*
skylight and, *35*
Statehouse Commissioners and, 11–12, 15, 17, 29, 51
State Room and, *74–75*
Thomas Cole sketch of, *10*, 11
ventilating stacks and, 18, *19*
wood carvings and, *28–29*
wood stairway and, *49*
The Ohio Statehouse Master Plan, 86
Ohio State Journal
 The Atrium and, 94, *95–96*,
 Capitol Festival and, *21*
 cows pasturing on the Ohio Statehouse grounds and, 106
 Grand Ovation and, 26
 iron fence enclosing the State House grounds and, 24
 Judiciary Building and, 86
 McKinley monument and, 103
 observation deck and, 49
 proposed Statehouse wing and, 85
 scaffolding in Rotunda and, 20
 squirrel house and, 106
 Statehouse Square and, 17
 unveiling of the *Lincoln and Soldiers' Monument* and, 42
 working on the Rotunda and, 23
Ohio Statesman, use of convicts for construction and, 17
Ohio Veterans Plaza, 112–113
Ohio Volunteer Infantry, 27
Ohio World War Memorial (Ivone), *110*
Ordinance of 1787, 15
Orville and Wilbur Wright and Their Accomplishments (Mutchler), *39*
Ott, Adelaide Sterling, 77

P

Pan-American Exposition, 103
Panic of 1893, 103
The Passing Show, *42*
Peace (Saville), *104–105*
Pedretti Brothers, 89
Pedretti, Charles, 87
Pedretti, Raphael, 86
Pelzer, Alphons, 111
Pemberton, John C., *40*
People's Room, 33
Perry, Oliver Hazard, 38
Perry's Victory (Powell), *38*
Persian Gulf War, 112
Philippine Insurrection, 108
Pigeon Run, 94, *95*
Pike, Jarvis, 7
The Plain Dealer, Ohio Veterans Plaza and, 112–113
Platt, William, 24
Pontifical College Josephinum, 111
Powell, William Henry, 38
presidential hearing rooms, *70*
Press and Broadcast News Rooms, 32–33

R

Randall & Aston's Book Stores, 21
Rat Row, 10
Report of the Superintendent of the Statehouse, dimensions of Statehouse and, 24, *25*
Reynolds, Arthur W., 110
Rhodes Tower, 87
Richard H. Finan Hearing Room, 87, *93*
Riffe Tower, 32
Robinson, John, 29
Rogers, Isaiah, 19–20, 44, 47, 62
Rollin, A.H., 60
Rosenberger, Clifford A., ix, *71*, 106, *107*

Rotunda, ix, 5, 18–21, 23–24, 26, *27*, 32, *33–36*, 37, 40, *42*
Royal Navy, 38
Rule, Charles, 58, 64
Rupert, Michael, 17, 28–29, 32, 51–52, 58, 62, 64, 66–69, 73, 77, 98
Rutledge, William, 3

S

Sailors and Soldiers Monument, 101
Samuel Hannaford & Sons, 86
Saville, Bruce Wilder, 104
Sawyer, J.O., 17
Schlesinger, George F., 108
Schooley Caldwell and Associates, 31–32, 86, 112
Schwartz, Michael, 118–119
Scioto River, 4, 13
Scofield, Levi T., 101
Scott, Maurice A., 12
Senate Caucus Rooms, 87, *92–93*
Senate Chamber, 18, *28*, *50*, *52*, 65–67
Senate Hearing Room, *90–91*
Shalev, Avner, 115
Shellenbarger, Dan, 17, 30–31, 37–39, 41, 59, 67, 71, 81, 86, 89, 91, 93, 98, 112
Sheridan, Philip H., *101–102*
Sherman, William T., *102*
The Signing of the Treaty of Greene Ville (Christy), *37*
Spanish-American War, 103, 108
Speaker's Chair, 60, *61*
Spirit of '98 (Jirouch), *108–109*
The Spirit of Life, 40
squirrel house, 106
Stanton, Edwin M., *102*
Starling, Lynn, 4

Statehouse Commissioners, 11–12, 15, 17, 29, 51
Statehouse Square, 7, 17
State Law Library, 87, *93*
State Library, 7, 29, 7
State Room, *74–75*
State Teacher's Retirement System, 98
St. Clair, Arthur, 37
St. Peter's Cathedral, 13
Sullivant, William, 13
Supreme Court, 18, 21, *28*, 32, 60, 85–87, *89–90*, *93*

T

Taft, William Howard, 70
The Talmud, 114
Taylor, W.A., 7
These Are My Jewels monument, *100–102*, *107*
Thomas J. Moyer Ohio Judicial Center, 87
Thompson, Carmi A., 108
Thompson, Charles F., 108
Thompson, Martin E., 11, 13
Tiffin, Edward, 5
toasts, 15
Toldeo Museum of Art, 12
Town, Ithiel, 12
Treaty of Greene Ville, 37

U

Ulysses S. Grant Presidential Hearing Room, *70*
United Spanish War Veterans Memorial Commission, 108
United States Supreme Court, 21
U.S. Marines, *36*, 112
U.S.S. Lawrence, 38
U.S.S. Niagara, 38

V

Van Wye, May Martin, 77
Vern Riffe State Office Tower, 32
Vicksburg, battle of, 40, 42
Vietnam War, 112

W

Waitt, Maude Comstock, 77
Waldsmith, Janet, 69
Waldsmith, John, 69
Walter, Henry, 11, 13, 16
War of 1812, 9, 13, 38
Watts, Eugene, 112
Wayne, Anthony, 37
Wells, William, 37
West, William Russell, 17, 29–20
W.H. Mullins studio, 111
William McKinley monument, *103–104*
Williams, George Washington, 76
Witt, John Henry, 26
Wolf Ridge, 6
Woman's Relief Corps of Ohio, 104
World's Columbian Exposition, 101
World War I, 82, 110
World War II, 112, 114
Worthington Center, 79, *81*
Worthington, Thomas, *5*, *7*, 106
Wright, Frank Lloyd, 32
Wright, Orville, *39*, 40, 98
Wright, Wilbur, *39*, 40, 98

Z

Zanesville state capitol building, *4*, *6*

About the Author

Chris Matheney at the annual American Revolutionary War living history day at the Ohio Statehouse, May 15, 2017. *Photo by Michael Rupert.*

CHRIS MATHENEY has a passion for early American history and recreates various characters from the French and Indian War through the American Revolution. In 1998, he portrayed Major Robert Rogers in the award-winning History Channel documentary *Frontier: Legends of the Old Northwest*, as well as contributing historical research to the Ohio PBS documentary *Opening the Door West*. Holding a degree in Interpretive Programs, Chris is the historic site manager of the Ohio Statehouse, serving fifteen years with the Ohio Historical Society before joining Capitol Square's Ohio Statehouse Museum Education Center. He lives in the foothills of Fairfield County, just outside of Lancaster, Ohio, with his lovely wife Wendy, and remarkable daughter Alana.